THE GAWLER FOUNDATION COO⌐

A RECIPE FOR LIFE 2

DOROTHY EDGELOW

THE GAWLER FOUNDATION COOKBOOK

A RECIPE FOR LIFE 2

DOROTHY EDGELOW

MICHELLE ANDERSON PUBLISHING
MELBOURNE

First published in Australia 2007
by Michelle Anderson Publishing Pty Ltd
P O Box 6032, Chapel Street North, South Yarra 3141, Melbourne, Australia
Tel: 03 9826 9028
Fax: 03 9826 8552
Email: mapubl@bigpond.net.au
www.michelleandersonpublishing.com

Cover design: Deborah Snibson, Modern Art Production Group
Photography: David Loram
Typesetting: Midland Typesetters, Australia
Printed by: Griffin Press, Adelaide

National Library of Australia cataloguing-in-publication data:

Edgelow, Dorothy
  The Gawler Foundation cookbook: a recipe for life.

  2nd ed.
  Includes index.
  ISBN 9780855723804.

  ISBN 0 85572 380 7.

  1. Cancer – Diet therapy – Recipes. 2. Cookery (Natural
  foods). I. Gawler Foundation. II. Title.

641.5631

Acknowledgments
A heartfelt thank you to all the many people who have been my inspiration and teachers over the years. My family and friends and over the last 25 years, the staff and the thousands of people who come to The Gawler Foundation. To the many who work in the healing professions, too many to name individually but all contributing to the information in this book one way or another. To nimble fingered computer people and brave publishers and you who use this book. May you all be truly blessed with health and happiness.

Dedication
To the spirit that gives us life and through that my family, my husband Ken and our daughters Lynette, Anne and Kerry and their husbands, our grandchildren and great grand-children who have given me all the joys this life can hold.

Thank you for choosing to share your life and love with me. May you receive in your lives all you have given me.

Dorothy Edgelow

CONTENTS

Introduction   1

The Gawler Foundation Services   6

The Gawler Foundation Dietary
    Principles and Practice   9

Cooking Techniques   13

Juices   16

Foods for Specific Systems of
    the Body   19

Useful Weights and Measures   22

Additives to Avoid   23

Shopping for Starters   25

Nutrients   26

Mono Diet   59

Acute or Healing Diet   60

Suggestions for 2-Week
    Healing Diet   62

Nutrient Charts   72

Maintenance Diet   78

Recipes: 80

    Vegetable   80

    Grains and Pulses   90

    Tofu   96

    Salads   98

    Soups   109

    Dressings   115

    Sauces   117

    Fish   119

    Bread   121

    Dips, Spreads and Stuffings   124

    Desserts   127

    Cakes   132

    Drinks   136

Thrive Natural Foods   138

FOREWORD

The Gawler Foundation has been helping people with cancer for over twenty-five years. There have been a wonderful group of therapists over those years and we have learnt so much about what works in practice – for example when people go home and actually prepare and eat food with the intention of supporting their health, their healing, their wellbeing and recovery. Of course we do study the literature – what is in the scientific journals as well as the popular press and books. However, there is no substitute for years of direct experience.

So one of The Foundation's strengths is this vast body of experience we have built up over the years. And Dorothy Edgelow has been at the forefront of this. Having helped her daughter use nutrition to overcome her own difficult cancer, Dorothy and her family went on to help establish The Foundation's residential program kitchen and menus. So now, Dorothy writes with the benefit of all that experience. Reading her book is like joining a wise old Grandmother (she actually is a great grandmother as well!) in the kitchen and gleaning her

wisdom. My wish is that you enjoy and benefit from the experience.

Just by way of further clarification, this book gives detail on what, at The Gawler Foundation, we call the Maintenance Diet, and the Healing Diet. Therefore, if healing is what you seek, be aware that you will need to be a little more thorough than if you are eating for maintenance or simply good basic health. Therefore, there is the need to discriminate regarding which recipes to use. This is clear in the way the book is set out with a section for both the Maintenance and the Healing diets.

Enjoy the book, the meeting with Dorothy, the recipes.

Enjoy eating well. Enjoy good health.

Ian Gawler OAM
Founder & Therapeutic Director
The Gawler Foundation
July 2007

INTRODUCTION

Miracles happen all the time. What is a miracle anyway? Something that happens that is outside a prediction or accepted way of perceiving a situation.

The miracle that changed my life was the recovery from a particular virulent cancer of one of our daughters. She had the conventional treatment that was used by the medical profession to treat her cancer, but the prognosis was not good. That was 28 years ago, she was well in six months and has no recurrence of cancer. We changed her diet, not to the level that is recommended now, just left out most meats and acidifying foods. Used some extra vitamins and minerals and tried to think positively that what she was doing would make her well. Lynette also had a very fervent wish to see her four-year-old and six-month-old sons grow up.

Searching for reasons for first developing cancer and then getting well, took us down many trails for many years. We learnt many of the practices that are accepted therapies now and eventually we opened four small restaurants serving wholesome food and through

those, met Dr Ian Gawler. On selling the business we volunteered our time to assist in the establishment of the now well-known Gawler Foundation.

Being where I am, I am privileged to see first-hand how the mind–body connection works. Both here at The Gawler Foundation and personally with myself and my family, many miracles have occurred. Full recovery from cancer, a baby predicted to be mentally retarded and was not. Also blood diseases usually causing death, blood and skin conditions that would usually require limb amputation, brain damage that disappeared and the birth of children when the parents were told it could not happen. They are part of my life story, along with my faith, the power of prayer and positive thinking.

In the seven years since producing *A Recipe for Life* much more evidence and research has been undertaken and has proven the ability of our minds and bodies to work together for our whole health. There are a number of conditions that need to be addressed in that search for health. Our minds are the prime movers to instigate this search. We need to believe that if we are given the right 'tools' in the form of information, these will allow us to make the right choices, which will lead us to a healthy, happy life.

Food is one of those tools. We can use it as one part of our medicine but we need to use good, clean food. Food that can supply life-giving nutrients to our body, not food that has been produced using more than 60,000 chemical additives to first make it grow and then to kill all life force in it so it can sit on a shelf for years without disintegrating. Any food that keeps looking good for many years needs to be viewed as a dead food. Embalmed, so to speak.

Apart from obvious illness in the physical body, irreparable damage can be done to the emotional, environmental and eventually spiritual body by the action of ingesting so much unbalanced food. Very rarely is a ready-made food with so-called healthy additives in balance. When a food is taken from its natural state and irradiated so as to not decompose, then have chemicals added to make it sound like a good product, it becomes exactly the opposite. How can a body be healthy when fed this way?

To start back on the road to health it is necessary to be aware of what you are putting in your mouth and the mouths of your family because you want them to be healthy too. There are many good books, much information from a huge array of avenues, many people who care about food willing to help us make informed choices when considering our health. Food is something we need to stay alive and so needs to be a priority in our lives. We have complete control of that part of our lives, we do have control of what we buy and eat, and there is always a choice. It is something we can do immediately and doing that, we start down the road to better health. Everything else we need to do becomes easier because our systems have decent fuel to work with.

Our body is the most marvellous complex piece of machinery ever devised and given a chance, will function perfectly. Put in simplified terms our physical body needs good food, our emotional body needs love, our mental body needs good positive thoughts, our physiological body needs understanding and our spiritual body needs acceptance, which when all in balance in the lives of all people, will help make this planet an even more beautiful place to be in.

Here at the Foundation we don't always remain in touch with those who come to learn, but there are many who contact us, maybe years after their visit here, to tell us of their changed lives and their good health. Everyone has an individual journey to complete and illness plays a role. Illness always happens for a reason, to alert us to something in our lives that is not good for us, something we need to learn from, an experience which allows us to go forward with a better level of health. We all need different solutions and by learning basic guidelines we can arrive at our own very personal and individual solutions. The information offered in the next pages will hopefully help you help yourself. I am still learning and I hope you are too.

While paying attention to what and how you eat is an important part of being healthy, the physical body does not function alone, we have developed past that. We as humans have been endowed with many more components. To be what is called healthy, all of those components should be recognised and used. Over the years, it seems to me controlling our health starts with the mind, the most powerful and motivating part of us. Having said that I must add that our acceptance of the spirit that gives us life, that gives us the experience of all that is here on earth, that allows us the joy of loving and caring, that makes us feel secure and gives us purpose in life is vitally important to our 'all over' health. To illustrate that point I would like to tell you a wonderful story.

About one year before writing this book, a perfectly healthy woman in her mid-fifties started to have pain in her hands and feet. Moving and inconsistent pains at times made it very difficult to walk and perform normal household tasks. Occasionally a rash appeared on her face and chest and she became disinterested in things around her. A visit to a doctor for tests was inconclusive, so a few natural therapies were tried, gaining some relief at times but the symptoms got worse.

She became less and less interested in food and consequently lost weight. This lady had always been a little unhappy with herself, expecting to do more with her time than she did. Had a couple of minor characteristic traits that she felt unable to change and as time went by became quite depressed. In three or four months she was unable to walk and felt better lying down in a fetal position. Her bodily functions were unstable and her whole body was in pain. On a visit to a specialist, he had her admitted to a large Melbourne hospital as he felt her life was in danger; as it was, she had developed jaundice as well.

Extensive examinations of all her systems showed everything was breaking down, collapsing, one system after another. The doctors treated all symptoms as they appeared and did many blood tests, biopsies, scans and were unable to find the cause of her deterioration.

After two days she was admitted to the intensive care unit and put on life support. Many procedures followed. Plasma exchange twice a day, blood transfusions, a dialysis machine was used together with intravenous fluids and oxygen, but with little response.

The family were told the worst news and waited as the doctors were unable to control the blood. One minute it would haemorrhage, next it would clot and the liver was enlarged and the pancreas inflamed. Meanwhile she was semi-conscious and a very strange dark-orange colour. The family were told she would not live through the night.

Thirty-six hours later on a wonderful morning, the blood stabilised and she was able to speak and got quite angry with the medical staff regarding the blood taken for tests and told the doctors so. None too politely, which was quite out of character. The next day she announced she was hungry. The procedures were all stepped up; food offered through a tube and a little strength returned and recognition of family and friends. A gradual improvement with many bad moments of slipping back, but a definite will to live was obvious.

Two weeks of incredible attention in ICU and to everyone's astonishment she was moving a little and was then sent to a general ward. Isolated at first, then into the general ward as she progressed. Low blood pressure and inability to pass fluids resulted in highly swollen legs and body. No protein in the blood and not able to move on her own. Good days and bad but a determination to get well. Little goals achieved each day. A wonderful day when her grandchildren were able to visit followed by being lifted out of bed into a chair. A few intravenous lines taken out but also lots of fluid off the lungs and many drugs for control of many malfunctions.

The only diagnosis of this had been a minor vague connection to a disease called Systemic Lupus Erythaematosus which is treated with drugs for the rest of one's life. This case was the worst ever seen by the medical staff and they had no explanation for the whole event, the speed of the decline nor of the incredible recovery. Two and a half months in hospital, four weeks in rehabilitation, learning to feed herself and walk again and then home. In only a couple of weeks she was back to normal life. Cooking, driving the car, baby-sitting grandchildren, flying away on short holidays, growing her hair and gradually cutting down medication. All the people who knew and loved her were convinced that her spirit was guiding and controlling her.

I was told that at one stage, the night her blood had stabilised, she had reached a point where she had to decide to live or die. To her it was a conscious decision, to leave this life and all she felt she could no longer deal with, or to try again. She decided to stay and then got back to the life she wanted very quickly. Each day a goal planned and achieved. Simple things like; today I move my fingers, tomorrow my arm, then lift my fork etc.

She now knows how powerful the mind, helped by the heart and spirit, can be and can overcome almost any problem. Once before this lady had shown how much power we have been given to help ourselves and others when she recovered from a diagnosis of terminal cancer, 27 years ago and remained very healthy until last year when she was tested again.

I am sure it happened for her to accept just what the human body and mind is capable of and as she doesn't like to talk about her achievements, she just does it as an example. I know this story to be as told; she is Lynette Archer, our daughter who once again has been a lesson to us all, of courage, strength and faith. In us all, if only we can believe it, is the ability to help ourselves.

Born with jaundice, back to being born again, jaundiced again, and having to learn all the human skills again, is another opportunity to remind us of the power of the mind.

THE GAWLER FOUNDATION SERVICES

LIFE AND LIVING—A 10-DAY
RESIDENTIAL FOR PEOPLE
DEALING WITH CANCER

Our bodies have a natural, inherent capacity to heal themselves. The principles that are explored in this program will enable you to activate and develop that healing power, maximising your body's potential to restore its natural state of balance and vitality. The principles include: relaxation and meditation; a positive state of mind; good diet and nutrition; overcoming obstacles to peace of mind; finding meaning and purpose in life and drawing upon effective support.

This is a self-help approach that is intended to work with and reinforce effective medical treatments as well as relevant complementary therapies.

The residential programs began in 1985. Many thousands of people have attended. This provides an amazing pool of shared knowledge, experience and diversity from teenagers to 80 year olds, from all walks of life, united by a common challenge. You can learn what has worked for many others and you will be helped to apply it in your own life.

The program requires a good deal of energy, so to benefit fully from attending you need to be able to join in. It is also important to read Ian's books before attending this program: *You Can Conquer Cancer*, *Peace of Mind*, *Meditation Pure and Simple* and *The Creative Power of Imagery*.

Most sessions involve learning through direct participation and experience. Discussion is encouraged and there is plenty of time for questions and answers. You can meet and share with a group of wonderful, exceptional people.

The Centre is spacious and comfortable, a wonderful environment for peace and healing. Some accommodation is shared with separate bathroom facilities, including a bathroom for the disabled. Twin rooms are available for couples, some with ensuites. Smoking is not permitted anywhere on The Foundation's 40-acre property.

The healthy, delicious meals are a direct translation of the principles in *You Can Conquer Cancer*. The food is organic (wherever possible), dairy-free, wheat-free, meat-free, fresh, abundant and vital. The Foundation offers a great range of beverages to complement the delicious vegan menu. Fresh juices are a feature of the program.

HEALTH, HEALING AND BEYOND

The 5-Day Follow-up Program, Health Healing and Beyond is suggested as a refresher course for those who have done the 10-Day Program. Health, Healing and Beyond has an informal and flexible format. A questionnaire is used to help identify the needs of each participant. Each program is tailored to meet those specific needs.

The program offers the opportunity for participants to refocus and go deeper into their healing process, to address any issues and obstacles they may have come up against, and to learn some new techniques. A major feature is the guided imagery work that introduces you to techniques that draw upon your inner wisdom and help you to develop insight and clarity.

It is also a chance to catch up with old friends, make new ones, to relax and to be taken care of—all in a peaceful and nurturing environment.

An ideal time to attend is six to 12 months after completing the initial 10-day residential program. Some people find it helpful to come back for a refresher every couple of years.

CANCER SELF-HELP PROGRAM

Our internationally acclaimed program has helped thousands of people with cancer and their families since 1981. Twelve weekly sessions focus upon a specific self-help theme based on themes from the book *You Can Conquer Cancer*. There is plenty of time to practise techniques as well as discussion and questions.

The program provides an opportunity to learn and discuss self-help techniques in a mutually supportive, positive and caring environment. The program is a two and a half hour session one day per week in Melbourne.

At The Foundation we recognize that support people, the relatives and friends of cancer patients, are often faced with major challenges of their own. What will happen? What can I do? Am I doing enough and doing it right? All these are very important questions for support people.

All The Foundation's programs are tailored to assist support people as well as patients, as they recognize the key role of both. Hence it is recommended that support people attend the groups and utilize the counsellor when needed.

CANCER SUPPORT GROUP

After completing the 12-week Cancer Self Help program or the ten day residential Life and Living program, you may join this weekly program which provides ongoing educational and social support for participants. The format focuses on sharing new ideas and experiences with others and reinforcing the principles of self-help, group meditation and mutual support.

LIVING IN BALANCE

This is a 5-day residential program designed to help you take time out for reflection and to recognize patterns in your life. Through letting go of old habits that no longer serve you well and integrating new and healthier strategies, you will experience a positive transformation in your daily life.

The program is a life-affirming program for people who recognize the need to reconnect with the essence of life – inner wisdom and strength. During this retreat you can journey inwards to explore meditation, imagery and effective emotional management skills, which you get to know yourself and draw upon the wiser parts of your being.

You can enjoy and learn about delicious, nutritious vegan food and relax in good company while you bask in the natural peace and tranquillity of the Yarra Valley.

MEDITATION RETREATS

These weekend retreats are designed to create harmony in the body, mind and spirit. It is a time to journey inward, to help you learn and practice techniques that will deepen your experience of meditation and to get to know your true self more closely. The focus is mainly experiential, with some discussion, and progresses from simple techniques through to more complex ones. During the program there is also plenty of time to enjoy the peace and beauty of the gardens and the Little Yarra River as it meanders through a forest of tall manna gums.

TAKING CONTROL OF MULTIPLE SCLEROSIS

This program has been developed and is facilitated by Professor George Jelinek and Dr Ian Gawler. The program based on George's book aims to: halt the progress of MS; create a sustainable life style program; introduce participants to self-help and self-healing techniques and address prevailing fears and misunderstandings about MS. The science is clear; people with MS who learn these techniques and integrate them with their medical management can reasonably hope to stabilise their condition.

COUNSELLING SERVICES

Our highly trained professional counsellors offer all aspects of general counselling. Major illness counselling, emotional and spiritual support for people nearing the end of their lives and support for families and friends.

CANCER SELF-HELP GROUPS— LEADERS' TRAINING

In-depth, residential training for people seeking endorsement to lead lifestyle-based cancer self-help groups. This program is based on the philosophy, materials and approach used in The Gawler Foundation's 12-week cancer self-help group program.

THE GAWLER FOUNDATION DIETARY PRINCIPLES AND PRACTICE

The principles behind The Foundation's choice of diet, is to take into our bodies food that is good for us. We recommend not eating dead or useless, filling foods or foods that are grown with or covered in chemicals. Our bodies have to cope with many external pollutants but we can control what goes into our mouths. We give our bodies a very definite message when we eat what we know is good for us. Even when we are not well, we should take an active part in choosing our food.

Organically grown fruit, vegetables and grains are now much more readily available. Biodynamically produced foods are too and effort needs to be made to obtain them. We are thereby making a definite effort to regain our health, from the mind through to the body.

When vegetables are grown well, they contain special enzymes that help to cleanse and build up the body. Serve grains with vegetables for complete nourishment, eating those that grow locally and are in season if you can. Eating raw vegetables and juices gives us certain nutrients, and cooking them allows us to access other properties not released when they are raw. A combination of two-thirds raw and one-third cooked is generally good.

Keeping your meals fairly simple, with not too many different ingredients in each meal helps toward better nutrition and absorption. If you cannot tolerate a lot of raw food, fresh juices can supply those enzymes and the vital forces usually gained through the eating of raw food. A few changes we can make quite easily in our kitchens will help eliminate unhealthy products and procedures which will in turn give our immune systems less work to do.

Our bodies need to be in a state of acid and alkaline balance (yin and yang in Chinese medicine), in order to be healthy. Animal foods, sugars and fats are generally acid-forming. Vegetables, grains and fruits are usually alkaline-forming. All natural foods contain both acid- and alkaline-forming elements in balance. If possible eat food close to its natural form. It is not the organic matter but the inorganic matter of foods that leaves acid residue in the body. Most grains can be acid-forming unless they are chewed very well. When chewing these, adding ptyalin from the saliva to the grain, in turn can change the acid element to alkaline.

Apart from food, our bodies are affected by our thoughts. There is a great deal of information about mind and body interaction, but in this book I will just say this: negativity, anger, resentment and unhappiness all affect how our bodies cope with food. Even the right type of food can be turned into an acid ash by these emotions. Try to relax and think calm happy thoughts when preparing and eating your meals.

If obtaining good organic food is difficult, buy the best fruit and vegetables you can and wash them in a solution of vinegar and water 1:100. Tell your body you are doing the best you can.

Here at the Centre we sit for a few moments of silence before each meal. We do not say a formal grace as it's not appropriate for everyone. Just take a moment or two to bless your food, be thankful for what you have and be positive that what you are eating and doing will help you to health.

To help you make decisions when choosing your food, take a look at Chinese principles and how the organs relate to one another. Take a look at the chemistry of food, at the nutritional aspect and also get to know and trust your own instincts. Buying, preparing and eating your good food should be a pleasure, not a chore. Find a way to enjoy it and you are well on the way to health. Remember that what you put in your mouth is only part of the way toward a healthy life. You must match it up with the other parts of your life. Sort out your past and present relationships with yourself and others. Sort out your emotional state and your spiritual beliefs and what has put you where you are. Accept that you are not expected to know everything and that your experiences are happening at the right time. There is no wrong time. We judge things to be right or wrong, good or bad. God does not. We feel guilt and judge ourselves and others. God does not.

CERTIFIED ORGANIC FOODS— WHY AND WHAT ARE THEY?
Organic food means food that has been produced using organic farming methods. Organic foods are grown without the use of pesticides, antibodies, hormones, artificial fertiliser, genetic manipulation, or any unnecessary exposure to environmental pollution. Even after the correct farming or growing procedures are practised, it takes quite a few years to be able to label produce 'certified organic'.

Although washing produce in a vinegar 1:100 solution does remove the outside sprays, a lot of damage is done to the actual seed before it goes into the ground, commonly known as Genetic Engineering.

A non-organic apple may have been dosed with up to 100 additives before you get to eat it. Broccoli generally has been sprayed with 32 chemicals. More than 50 per cent of all pesticides sprayed on fruit and vegetables are there merely to improve its appearance. Organically grown food is sometimes smaller and less attractive, with a few blemishes, but the flavour and nutrient content are far superior. Many of the chemicals used to spray crops have been linked to allergies and cancer. Some are associated with Irritable Bowel Syndrome, Candida and Inflammatory Bowel Disease and lowered fertility. Apart from being better for our health, organic farming is better for our planet too.

WHAT IS BIODYNAMICS?
Biodynamics is an advanced form of organic agriculture, which was introduced by Dr Rudolf Steiner in 1924. Dr Steiner was an Austrian scientist/philosopher who had deep insight into nature and into many areas of human endeavor. He gave detailed suggestions for a renewal of agriculture in a series of lectures given to farmers in 1924. He insisted that all his suggestions were fully tested and scientifically validated. This sound scientific basis continues to be an important feature of bio-dynamics today.

The method spread rather slowly worldwide. In the 1950s, Alex Podolinsky made it applicable to large acreage and small workforce farms in Australia, thus appealing to the many professional farmers who felt morally ill at ease with the use of artificial fertilisers and poisonous sprays. Podolinsky's group, the Bio-dynamic Agricultural Association of Australia, is now the largest natural farming body anywhere in the world. Members produce every type of product that can be grown in Australia on farms totalling many million hectares.

Biodynamic methods and equipment created in Australia are now used in many countries and Alex advises farmers in Europe, Scandinavia, the Ukraine, America and South Africa.

Biodynamic Features
500 is a substance made from specially controlled cow manure, taking many months to prepare. It is liquefied and sprayed on the soil twice a year. It creates a powerful soil structure, promoting humus formation and root growth.

Companion Planting
Different plant species interact with each other in a variety of ways. Some combinations have been found to be beneficial, some to produce negative results. Biodynamic growers try to select suitable combinations of plants for best results, to improve flavour and nutrients and lessen destructive bugs and soil damage.

Sowing by the Moon and Zodiac
Biodynamic practitioners follow a sowing chart developed as a result of careful research carried out over many years. It is quite different from popular magazine charts and is not based on folklore or mysticism. By sowing seed according to this chart, a biodynamic gardener/farmer can influence plants to grow more root, leaf, flower or fruit and produce substantially better crops.

Other features of biodynamic practice are available by contacting the Biodynamic Gardeners Association and Biodynamic Resource Centre, PO Box 479, Leongatha VIC 3953, telephone (03) 5664 9219.

B.D.F.G.A.A. (Biodynamic Farmers and Gardeners Association of Australia)
PO Box 54
Bellingen NSW 2454

Bio-dynamics Tasmania
PO Box 177
St Marys TAS 7217
(03) 6372 2211

Organic Federation of Australia
Website: www.ofa.org.au
Canberra Organic Growers Society
www.netspeed.com.au/cogs.htm
Organic Association of Australia
Hotline: 1800 356 299

COOKING CLASSES
The current food regulations class the Foundation as Category A which does not allow it to offer cooking classes on the premises. We can however, suggest Michelle Russell (Thrive Natural Foods). Details at end of Recipe section.

COOKING TECHNIQUES

Cooking without meat, dairy products, fats and a minimum of sugars and salts is, to some, an enormous challenge. Once you are comfortable with the basic techniques, there is a great freedom to eating this way. Limiting the variety of ingredients that you use in your meals each day allows you a bigger variety throughout a week.

One of the major factors in feeling satisfied after eating is to have a good balance of nutrients in your meal and not just vegetables. You can achieve this by having grain in some way with each meal, ie. porridge at breakfast, bread in some form at lunch and any of the grains made into pasta or in natural form at dinner. Any of the pulses are also good at filling that gap that people using vegetable diets sometimes feel; the need for something more that sends them to the sweets department in the kitchen.

Remember that nutrients are lost when food is reheated so it is better to buy your fresh ingredients and cook at mealtimes rather than pre-cooking. There is a risk of exposing yourself to bad bacteria when pre-heated food is used.

Tests done by government health departments now show that one of the most dangerous things to do with grains and vegetables is to keep them for more than 24 hours. Bacteria can grow even in the fridge. Freezing destroys many nutrients as does the use of microwaves. Microwaves also produce free radicals. For at least six months you need to take all the precautions you can to ensure your body has a chance to rebuild without having to fight the invasion of poisons and toxins. Make sure everything you put in your mouth is helping you to health.

Steaming, dry baking and boiling are the best ways to cook. Use stainless steel, glass or non-chipped enamel pots, pans and utensils. Do not use aluminium pots, or aluminium foil to cover or wrap your food. Covering can be done with a lid or another tray. Store in glass jars or stainless bowls—no plastic if possible. Covering can also be done with greaseproof paper held in place with a string or rubber band. Even a plate on top of a bowl works. One food can contaminate another, particularly cooked and raw food stored together uncovered in the fridge. Greaseproof paper can be used in place of plastic-wrap. Also use greaseproof paper to wrap food in small portions if you have to freeze some.

Use a wooden chopping board in preference to a plastic, glass or laminated one. Wood has quite a few advantages. When properly looked after by scrubbing after use, then rinsed off in boiling water, it will not harbour germs. It is now suggested that the plastic boards harbour more bacteria then wooden ones. Wood also saves your very expensive knives from damage. Glass and laminate kill the edges of your knife, so please go to the trouble of looking after your wooden board. It's best to have two or three boards. One for fruit, one for ordinary vegetables and one for the onion-garlic family.

Enjoyment of food and the way you eat is an expression of who you are. Enjoyment of good food and company creates such an inner joy that it is possible to taste the sweetest of nectar in even the simplest of food. Without this joy, and with no blessing offered, the most wholesome, delicious food can seem tasteless and leave the soul hungry. People who eat only for the taste and who do not look at nutritional value often develop cravings for something they aren't getting. They bring turmoil into their lives and homes in their constant search, and they eat to satisfy a misplaced hunger. But do not become so rigid or self-righteous about your diet as to annoy others. A bad relationship with yourself or others is more poisonous than a bad diet. If you desire a 'treat', it is better to have it than stuff yourself with rice to try to suppress the desire.

Set aside a special time and place for meals in a clean environment, surrounded with pleasant sounds, aromas, colours and conversation. Avoid emotionally charged subjects and confused, scattered talk or thoughts. Avoid eating while tired, too hot or too cold, worried, angry, standing, watching TV, reading or before bathing. These activities make the food hard to digest. Relax and get comfortable. Perhaps undertake self-reflection about your health. Eating is a time to receive offerings in the form of food that nurtures and revitalises your body. Consider your manners insofar as they represent your attitude to others. Give attention to the unique qualities of each food and the work involved in bringing it to you.

Relax after eating, but do not fall asleep or into a stupor. Relaxation helps you digest your food and sleep well at night.

Give thanks before and after eating.

Choose the majority of your foods from local growers if possible. (This helps your health, and your local economy as well as the environment by using fewer resources for shipping and refrigeration.)

Liquids and food should not be too hot or too cold. This is especially important for infants and children. Heat debilitates the stomach and creates acidity. Cold paralyses it by slowing down the digestive enzyme action.

Drinking with meals dilutes the digestive juice. However, a small amount of warm water or green tea—100 ml or less—is acceptable. In general, drink water.

The minimum recommended amount of liquid required by a body is two litres per day from all sources. Include juices and teas in this amount.

JUICES

Raw juices are rich in vitamins, minerals, trace elements and enzymes. These very necessary elements are easily assimilated into the bloodstream without putting a strain on the digestive system, which is always under stress when we are ill. The nutritive elements in juices are beneficial in normalising body processes. They supply much-needed elements to activate all regeneration. Juices of vegetables have an alkalising effect on the blood helping to bring the pH back to the right acid/alkaline balance.

Mineral imbalance in the tissues is one of the causes of lack of oxygen in the body, which can lead to disease. Raw juices help our bodies to expel toxins by breaking down and disposing of old dying cells, then revitalising the active cells thus leading to the building of new healthy cells.

Juices should be consumed slowly, sipping and mixing the juice with the saliva in the mouth. The most benefit is gained by drinking the juice within 10 minutes of preparing and taking 10 minutes to drink it. Try not to use more than four vegetables in a juice. Sometimes diarrhoea results when you start to take a number of fresh juices, and as long as it is not too severe, don't be concerned as this is nature doing a little house cleaning. Possibly you will lose a little weight but this will be regained in time by the rebuilding of your body.

If you don't mix fruit and vegetables together you will gain more from your juice as fruits digest faster than vegetables and then they have to wait around for the vegetables to be processed and in that time, they start to ferment and can be one of the causes of gas problems.

Carrots can be mixed with most other vegetables and are one of the most commonly used juices. Carrots with celery and parsley—use 70% carrot. Carrots with beetroot—use 80% carrot. Carrots with parsley and garlic—use 98% carrot.

A juice made of fresh green leaves is full of chlorophyll. The great bowel cleanser. A dirty bowel gives rise to dirty blood. Only use the outer dark-green leaves of lettuce, a few spinach or silver beet leaves, some cabbage leaves and a little celery or green capsicum will make a great cleansing juice. You can add a spoonful or two of a powdered green supplement, if you wish to make a more potent juice. The green powders are very beneficial and can be used in water on their own if it's not convenient for you to make a fresh leafy green juice.

Certain cancer diets recommend over 12 juices per day but at the Centre we serve on average seven. One of the reasons for this is time. The diet that recommends 12 juices is very specific and requires a total commitment to a food program as well and can be physically exhausting because of the time required to prepare it. At The Gawler Foundation juices are served between meals and programs. As they are highly beneficial food they should be consumed on their own.

Bottled and tinned juices are not as nutritious as freshly made ones. If you need to make several juices at one time, put the juices in a small thermos or bottle, filling it to the top and keep it as cool as possible and in the dark. Juices are absorbed in 20 minutes so will not cause as much digestive complication due to fermentation as would happen when the same vegetables are eaten together in a salad. You should chew all foods well, even a juice, as they are really a food. Also consuming them on an empty stomach is better. Juices are of more benefit when drunk in small quantities, 100–200 ml at a time.

Eating live foods results in vibrant cells which create a vibrant healthy body. The sun's rays activate the enzymes in grown foods. Live foods fuel us with this life force present in their enzymes and nutrients. Those nutrients cleanse the body of accumulated toxins and wastes.

JUICES RECOMMENDED FOR A HEALING DIET

*Lemon Juice and Water: Vitamin C—*First thing in the morning. Prepares and cleanses and helps to clear the mucus from the body, particularly the liver.

*Carrot Juice: Vitamin A—*Repairs tissue and cell damage. A strong antiseptic. Also contains Vitamins B1, B2 and C which aid in strengthening the nervous system.

*Beetroot and Carrot—*Cleanses the liver and is a blood builder.

*Green Juice: Lettuce: Iron. Celery: Sodium and Calcium. Capsicum: Vitamin C. Cabbage: Vitamin A. Parsley: Chlorophyll, Vitamin A and Sodium. Spinach: Vitamin A and Iron—*Blend any combination together or use *Barley Green—*a powder made from the shoots of young barley. It has many properties and is the highest source of chlorophyll, which builds the blood enhancing the immune system. One teaspoon of Barley Green in water or could be added to green juice.

*Grape Juice—*Blood builder and high in Iron.

Apple Juice—Eliminates body toxins and cleanses the liver and kidneys. *Pear Juice*—Is great to clear constipation. Choose only one of any fruit juice every few days.

7 × approx 200 ml glasses of juice daily as per recommendation:

¼ glass lemon juice and ¾ glass water — warm

2 glasses plain carrot juice

1 glass carrot and celery juice (⅔ glass carrot and ⅓ celery juice)

2 glasses carrot, celery and beetroot juice (½ carrot, ¼ celery, ¼ beetroot)

1 glass green juice (approx ⅓ glass each, cabbage, lettuce and celery, adding 3–4 tbs green capsicum juice and 1 tsp barley green powder)

These 7 juices give you these nutrients daily:

Calories	Protein	Calcium	Carbohydrates
641 gr	38 gr	1063 mg	243 gr

Calories	RDA* Women	1850 gr	RDA Men	2600 gr
Protein	RDA Women	44–48 gr	RDA Men	56–65 gr
Calcium	RDA Women	800 mg	RDA Men	800 mg
Carbohydrates	RDA Women	277 gr	RDA Men	390 gr

*RDA = recommended daily average

Compare the nutrients from the seven juices taken daily, and recommended by The Foundation with the RDA of the same nutrients.

<u>This is only a brief outline of the properties that the juices contain. For further reading refer to:</u> *The Uses of Juices* by CE Clinkard. *Foods that Heal* by Dr Bernard Jensen. *Green Barley Essence* by Yoshihide Hagiwara M.D.

FOODS FOR SPECIFIC SYSTEMS OF THE BODY

Respiratory System
Specific nutrients needed to nourish this system:
- Vitamins: A, all Bs, C, D, E, inositol, niacin, folic acid, pantothenic acid and bioflavonoids
- Minerals: calcium, iron, silicon, potassium, magnesium and copper
- Foods: onion family, garlic, green leafy vegetables, grapes, pears and pineapple

Digestive System
Specific nutrients needed to nourish this system:
- Vitamins: A, all Bs, C, D, E, F, folic acid, inositol, niacin and pantothenic acid
- Minerals: magnesium, potassium, iron, sulphur, copper and zinc
- Foods: Lots of green leafy vegetables, watercress, beetroot and some soured milk products eg. yoghurt

The Circulatory System
Specific nutrients needed to nourish this system:
- Vitamins: all Bs, E, folic acid and bioflavonoid
- Minerals: calcium, iron, silicon, magnesium, phosphorous, zinc, potassium, nitrogen and sulphur
- Foods: lentils, buckwheat, alfalfa, whole rice, brewers yeast, sprouted grains, beetroot, rye, sardines, liquid chlorophyll, omega-3 oil and lots of fresh vegetables

The Central Nervous System
Specific nutrients needed to nourish this system:
- Vitamins: A, B, C, D, E, F, folic acid and niacin, B vitamins in wholegrains (plus oats, rice and wheatgerm), wild blue-green algae and cabbage, really strengthen the nerves
- Minerals: calcium, phosphorous, magnesium, iron, sulphur, iodine, potassium and zinc

Magnesium foods help to calm the nerves, as does dill, basil and chamomile tea, while calcium helps them to function in the body
- Foods: fish, raw goats milk, egg yolk, nutritional yeast, (chicken, meat and dairy—can use when well in small amounts only)

Skeletal System

Specific nutrients needed to nourish this system:

- Vitamins: approx. 20 minutes per day of sunshine (vitamin D) with maximum body trunk exposure
- Minerals: calcium, zinc, iron, potassium, magnesium and sodium
- Foods: grains, almonds, lots of yellow vegetables and some good-quality protein from legumes (not much sugar as sweet foods retard calcium metabolism)

Muscular System

Specific nutrients needed to nourish this system:

- Vitamins: A, B complex, C, D, E, biotin, choline and pantothenic acid
- Minerals: calcium, potassium, magnesium, silicon, nitrogen and iron
- Foods: all grains, lima beans, sprouts and fish (NB: too much protein causes loss of calcium by way of urine)

Immune or Lymphatic System

Specific nutrients needed to nourish this system:

- Vitamins: A, all Bs, C, biotin, folic acid, choline and pantothenic acid
- Minerals: potassium and sodium
- Foods: green leafy vegetables, apple, celery and watercress

Endocrine System

Specific nutrients needed to nourish this system:

- Vitamins: B complex, C, E, inositol, folic acid and pantothenic acid
- Minerals: iodine, silicon, phosphorous, calcium, magnesium, sodium, iron and potassium
- Foods: lecithin, sea vegetables, green vegetables, eggs, seeds and nuts

The Integument (Skin) System

Specific nutrients needed to nourish this system:

- Vitamins: A, B complex, C, D, E, F, K, pantothenic acid, folic acid, niacin and bioflavonoid
- Minerals: silicon, calcium, fluorine, iron, sulphur, iodine, copper, manganese, zinc and magnesium
- Foods: rice, sea vegetables, whey, millet, sprouts, avocado, apple, cucumber and raw goat's milk

Urinary System

Specific nutrients needed to nourish this system:

- Vitamins: A, B complex, C, D, E, and pantothenic acid
- Minerals: calcium, potassium, manganese, silicon, iron and magnesium
- Foods: liquid chlorophyll, green leafy vegetables, parsley, asparagus, apple and watermelon

Excretory System

Specific nutrients needed to nourish this system:

- Vitamins: A, all Bs, E, folic acid and niacin

- Minerals: magnesium, sulphur, calcium, iron and sodium
- Foods: green leafy vegetables (chlorophyll), yoghurt and all soured milk products, well cooked grains, flaxseed, sprouted seeds and all types of squash

Reproductive System
Specific nutrients needed to nourish this system:
- Vitamins: A, B complex, C, D, E and F

- Minerals: zinc, calcium, iodine, phosphorous, iron, sodium, potassium and silicon
- Foods: Some seeds (including pumpkin and nut butters), egg yolk, lecithin and raw goat's milk.

There is now much evidence to show that live nutrients from food, not from synthetic tablets, produce a much better result in the body.

USEFUL WEIGHTS AND MEASURES

One cup of Dry Weight in . . .
Almonds equals 200 g
Apricots equals 200 g
Barley equals 150 g
Beans equals 200 g
Brown Rice equals 200 g
Buckwheat equals 250 g
Carob Buds equals 150 g
Carob Powder equals 100 g
Chickpeas equals 150 g
Coconut equals 100 g
Couscous equals 150 g
Currants equals 125 g
Dates equals 150 g
Flour Rice equals 150 g
Flour Soy equals 100 g
Flour Wholemeal equals 150 g
Great North Beans equals 200 g
Lentils equals 250 g
Lima Beans equals 150 g
Millet equals 250 g
Oat Bran equals 100 g
Polenta equals 200 g
Raisins equals 150 g
Semolina equals 200 g
Soy Compound equals 100 g

Split Peas equals 150 g
Sultanas equals 150 g
Unprocessed Bran equals 100 g
Wild Rice equals 200 g

Liquid Measures
Millilitres/Cups and Spoons
5 ml 1 Teaspoon (tsp)
20 ml 1 Tablespoon (tbs)
250 ml 1 cup
600 ml 2½ cups
1 litre 4 cups

Weight equivalents
Metric/Imperial
30 g 1 oz
100 g 3½ oz
500 g 16 oz
1000 g 2.2 lbs

Oven Temperatures
Slow 150°C
Moderate 180°C
Hot 200–210°C
Very Hot 230°C

ADDITIVES TO AVOID

The following list includes those additives in food products that are known to have links with allergies and reactions.

ARTIFICIAL COLOURS
E102 Tartrazine
E104 Quinoline Yellow
E107 Yellow 2G
E110 Sunset Yellow
E120 Cochineal
E122 Carnosine
E123 Amaranth
E124 Ponceau 4R
E127 Erythrosine
E128 Red 2G
E129 Allura Red
E132 Indigo Carmine
E133 Brilliant Blue
E142 Green S, Food Green, Acid Brilliant Green
E150 Caramel
E151 Black PN
E154 Brown FK
E155 Chocolate Brown HT

NATURAL COLOUR
E160b Annatto

PRESERVATIVES
200–203 Sorbic Acid, Potassium and Calcium Sorbates
210–213 Benzoic Acid, Sodium, Potassium and Calcium Benzoates
220–228 Sulphur Dioxide, all Sulphites, Bisulphate's, Metabisulphites
249–252 All Nitrates and Nitrites
280–283 Propionic Acid, Sodium, Potassium and Calcium Propioriates

ANTI-OXIDANTS—used to extend the life of some processed packaged foods.
E211 Sodium Benzoate
E310 Propyl gallate
E311 Octyl gallate
E312 Dodecyl gallate
E319 TBHQ
E320 Butylated hydroxyanisole
E321 Butylated hydroxytoluene

FLAVOUR ENHANCERS
620 Glutamic acid eg. MSG
621 Sodium hydrogen L-glutamate (Monosodium glutamate; MSG)
622 Potassium hydrogen L-glutamate
623 Calcium dihydrogen di-L-glutamate
624 Glutamic acid eg. MSG

625 Glutamic acid eg. MSG
627 Guanosine 5"-(disodium phosphate)
631 Ompsome 5"-(disodium phosphate)
635 Sodium 5"-ribonucleotide

SWEETENERS

951 Aspartane—generally used to sweeten products labeled 'sugar-free'—can have potentially damaging side-effects and are worse for the body than sugar.

SHOPPING FOR STARTERS

Basic foods that you can keep on hand to use in the preparation of a healthy diet.

Dry Goods

Agar Agar
Almonds
Apple Cider Vinegar
Apple Juice
Barley Green Powder
Barley Miso
Barley Rolled
Brown Rice
Buckwheat Kernels
Carob Powder
Chickpeas
Cold Extracted Flax Oil
Corn Flour
Corn Noodles
Currants
Dandelion Coffee Grounds
Green Tea
Haricot Beans
Herb Teas of your choice
Herbamare
Honey
Hulled Millet
Jam (unsugared)
Kelp Powder

Kombu
Lentils
Maple Syrup
Mayonnaise Soy
Mustard English
Oats Rolled
Olives Black
Polenta
Prunes
Rice Crackers
Rice Flour
Rice Pasta
Rice Rolled
Rice Syrup
Salt Skip (Baking Powder substitute)
Slippery Elm Powder
Split Peas
Sultanas
Sundried Tomatoes
Sushi Nori
Tamari
Tomato Puree
Triticale Rolled
Unpearled Barley
Vanilla (pure)
Whole Linseeds
Wholemeal Flour
Yellow Split Peas

NUTRIENTS

PROTEINS

Proteins are components of all cells. They stick everything together and are necessary for the growth of all internal organs and for the quality of the muscles, blood, hair and nails. They are made up of a large number of amino acids.

One plant food may not contain all the necessary amino acids, but if we have a good mix of vegetables and grains we obtain all the essential amino acids. Too much protein results in many conditions that lead to illness. Proteins in all forms are acid to our system and in excess can cause excessive weight gain, dehydration, cancer and many other problems. The residue of meat fibre left after basic digestion is a major cause of bowel problems as our bowel is very long and meat fibre putrefies very quickly, getting stuck along the way. Fish, grains and legumes are a better choice of protein. Sea vegetables are also good sources of protein and have the advantage of being processed in the system without side effects. Dairy (milk and cheese) because of the processing that they are put through, are quite useless to the system. There are nutrients in dairy milk but the human system cannot access them. We do not have a number of stomachs as calves do.

Protein Foods
- Fresh nuts (but not peanuts as they contain aflotoxins which are a carcinogenic fungus resulting from the chemical spraying of the soils, essential for growing peanuts)
- All sea vegetables—nori, arame, hijike, kelp, kombu, agar agar
- Fish—preferably deep-sea fish
- Soy products—tofu, tempeh, yoghurt, milk, flour, tamari
- Lentils
- Chickpeas
- Lima and Kidney beans
- Barley
- Alfalfa
- Meat, chicken
- Corn
- Dairy—milk, cheese, yoghurt, keffir
- Bread—small amount in some breads.

Vegetables and fruits have minimal protein content but are an essential part of a balanced diet. Often, people are concerned that eating a vegetarian diet means they are not supplying enough protein, but if you check the charts you will see that protein is easy to obtain.

Protein required:

Adult:	Women	44–50 grams daily
	Men	55–65 grams daily
Child (3–7 yrs):		26–50 grams daily
Infant (1 yr):		3 grams daily

CARBOHYDRATES

Carbohydrates come in two forms: complex and simple.

Complex Carbohydrates

Our bodies function better when most of our carbohydrate intake is in the form of what are called complex carbohydrates which are found in grains, legumes, seeds, nuts, vegetables and fruit. The components of carbohydrates are starch, sugar and cellulose (or fibre). During digestion, the carbohydrates from these foods are broken down and transformed into glucose. Some of this 'blood' sugar is used as fuel for the brain tissue, nervous system and muscles. This type of carbohydrate also regulates protein and fat metabolism. The starches in carbohydrate foods are assimilated slowly to help keep the glucose level in the blood constant. Fibre is essential for correct functioning of the bowel and elimination processes.

Carbohydrates are needed for energy but can be converted to fat by the body. Complex carbohydrates can be burned by the body to produce energy. Protein is also needed and used by the body for energy and if the right kind of carbohydrates are ingested, the protein is freed from the job of producing energy and can concentrate on other needs. Carbohydrates can be a problem if too many are eaten, particularly in the form of pasta. These types of carbohydrates give a quick boost of energy because they are converted to a type of sugar. Most pastas are so highly refined and processed that there is no other nutrient of lasting value left in the product.

Simple Carbohydrates

Simple carbohydrates (plain sugar) give a short energy boost and then deplete the body of other nutrients. They are found in all baked goods such as cakes, buns and biscuits, and sweetened foods, drinks and confectionery. If you are concerned about your weight it is useful to know that, according to some medical studies, the digestion of carbohydrates slows down after 4 pm. Your 'Biological Clock' does this. Food that is not properly digested is stored as fat by the body.

CALCIUM

Calcium is a very necessary mineral needed by almost all parts of the body to function correctly. Calcium can be obtained from sources other than dairy and can be 'manufactured' or increased by the body if some vitamin D (sunshine) is available. Calcium can also be supplied by some of the green leafy vegetables, sprouted seeds or grains and sea vegetables.

Vegetables and grains also contain calcium. Exercise in all forms helps the body to develop even more calcium. Sea vegetables (seaweeds) are becoming more familiar to those in western society and contain very large amounts of almost all the nutrients that humans need. Seaweeds are an excellent source of calcium and minerals as well as protein and iodine, which we need in small amounts to balance our thyroid action. These sea vegetables can be soaked and then chopped small and mixed in with other foods if the flavour needs to be disguised. Only small amounts of sea vegetables are needed to make a big difference to our health.

Unless food is able to be chewed well (to incorporate the saliva), the nutrients in any food will not be completely assimilated. As dairy is acidic to the body and can contribute to pH imbalance, many children and some adults develop a condition called lactose intolerance from the use of cow's milk and its by-products. In the past, whole untreated milk did not cause as many problems as the highly processed milk and milk products of today do. These modern products are out of balance, can be difficult to digest with their extra additives, and the fats needed for assimilation are taken out. The many processes that are used to give milk a longer shelf life do not allow the product to be as beneficial as it could be in its natural state. Natural yoghurt from any milk is usually assimilated well, and you can add your own fruit when needed. Those who can't tolerate milk can usually handle soured or fermented milk products. Soy, oat, rice and almond milk are all sources of calcium. These milks can be made at home if they are preferred to commercial varieties.

VITAMINS

Vitamins are not able to be produced by our bodies and so have to be ingested from a well-balanced diet. There are 13 essential vitamins and others that are only needed in minute amounts. Fat soluble vitamins A, D, E, and K can be stored by the body to be used as needed. Water soluble vitamins B5, C, Biotin, Folic acid and Pantothenic acid cannot be stored and need constant renewal as any excess is excreted through urine and perspiration. Deficiencies could lead to:

Vitamin A
—Bronchial infection and problems in the respiratory tract
—Blurred vision and other eye problems
—Difficulty digesting fats
—Rickets (softening of the bones)

Vitamin B1

—(Thiamine) Crohns Disease, Ulcerative Colitis
—Depression, confusion, poor appetite
—Swelling of the ankles and feet
—Inability to concentrate

Vitamin B2

—(Riboflavin) Intolerance to bright light
—Mouth ulcers, scaling around the nose, ears, mouth and forehead
—Inflammations, inability to urinate
—Lack of concentration, depression

Vitamin B3

—(Niacin) Arthritis, arteriosclerosis
—Headaches and general tiredness
—General irritation of digestive mucous membranes

Vitamin B5

—(Pantothenic Acid) Low blood sugar
—Adrenal and muscular exhaustion
—Decrease in antibody formation
—Muscular cramps

Vitamin B6

—(Pyridoxine) Anaemia, convulsions, migraine
—Fluid retention, cramps, constipation
—Parkinson's disease

Vitamin B12

—Mental slowness and disturbances, pernicious anaemia, herpes
—Glandular fever, anorexia, unpleasant body odor

Folic Acid

—Leukemia, anaemia, arterioscleroses
—Mental and physical tiredness

Choline

—High cholesterol levels
—High blood pressure, loss of hair
—Heart palpitations, visual disturbances, liver and kidney problems

Vitamin D

—Rickets in children, poor metabolism
—Tetany (muscular membrane flabbiness)

Vitamin E

—Problems with the reproductive and circulatory systems
—Reduction of oxygen and nutrient transportation in the body

MINERALS

There are at least fifteen minerals needed in minute amounts for health. Sometimes, when a diet is low in good-quality fruit, vegetables and grains, supplements are needed but advice should be sought from a qualified practitioner.

Calcium	Sodium
Iodine	Copper
Potassium	Magnesium
Chlorine	Sulphur
Iron	Fluorine
Silica	Phosphorous
Chlorophyll	Zinc
Manganese	

Minerals and trace elements are vital to our health. But not much information is offered about these nutrients when diet is discussed and planned. Perhaps because they are needed only in minute amounts. Minerals and trace elements are responsible for important enzyme reactions in the body. Their actions are subtle but very effective. Not a lot is understood about the processes these trace elements are involved in but unless we ingest them in our food or water, our health will suffer. Minerals and trace elements are only available to us if the soil that is used to grow these foods contains essential nutrients. Overuse and fertilisation of soil destroys them. Sea water and sea vegetables can provide the minerals needed by humans and now there are many products from the sea that we are able to use to supplement our diet.

A brief description of minerals is as follows:

Carbon

The principle element for growth, carbon oxygen and hydrogen work together in our body in many of the processes of our cells in bones, cartilage, skin, organs, glands and tissue. Carbon is plentiful in all the foods we eat.

Hydrogen

The main element of acidification and working with oxygen forms the molecule of alkalisation. Hydrogen is in all foods, the air and water we drink. Like oxygen it is a life-giving element.

Calcium

Calcium is a healing element. It gives vitality, endurance, heals wounds and neutralises acids. It works with Vitamin D, phosphorus and magnesium in bone structure. But it is necessary to have manganese, copper and zinc together in order for calcium to be deposited in the bones.

Nitrogen

Is essential for human and animal life for building tissue. Nitrogen is a constituent of protein and is plentiful in nature and in the air we breathe.

Phosphorus

Is needed by the bones, brain and nerves. Some of its work is to transform stores of glycogen into glucose to stabilise blood sugar levels. The brain needs animal phosphorus rather than vegetable phosphorus to function at its deep-thinking level.

Chlorine

Works mainly in the digestive system and its secretions. Chlorine expels waste. Lack of chlorine causes sluggish liver and swollen glands. Chlorine works with sodium in the blood and in stimulation of muscle tissue.

Sulphur

Sulphur is a building element important to the glands and sexual system. Our immune system needs sulphur. The brain, nervous system, skin, nails and hair also use sulphur.

Potassium

Potassium and its partner sodium have many functions to perform in the body. In neutralising acidic metabolic wastes, regulating osmotic pressure, controlling the acid/alkaline balance in the body and in heart support.

Sodium

This element is a ligament, gland and blood builder. It is needed to keep calcium in solution so calcium does not deposit in the bone joints causing spurs. Sodium is found in the stomach where it naturalises the stomach acids at appropriate times.

Fluorine

Fluorine is a natural germicide. It strengthens bones and aids resistance to disease. Usually plentiful in soil and plants but is destroyed by heat in cooking. Raw goat's milk is high in fluorine.

Magnesium

Magnesium is found in muscles, soft organs and fluids. It regulates the heart muscle. Magnesium activates enzymes that are involved with the energy system of cells. It helps regulate body temperature and assists in the making of protein.

Silicon

Silicon is found in hair, nails, teeth and ligaments. Silicon is responsible for sparkling eyes, good hearing and glossy hair. A person with ample silicon loves to be moving and doing things.

Iron

Iron promotes vitality and ambition. Iron is taken from food through the blood vessels to the bone marrow where haemoglobin is made. Reserves of iron are in the liver and muscle tissue in the form of ferriten. Lack of iron is a major cause of fatigue and can lead to anaemia.

Iodine

Iodine is usually plentiful in vegetables from the sea and those grown on land close to the sea. The thyroid needs iodine to function properly. Iodine deficiency in children can result in slow mental and physical development. The thyroid regulates the metabolism throughout the body.

Manganese

Manganese is a memory element. A tissue strengthener needed for bone formation and many enzyme actions. Manganese, copper, calcium and zinc used together can help prevent osteoporosis.

These elements are specifically needed by certain body organs.

Thyroid	—Iodine
Bowel	—Magnesium
Bowel/Nervous System	—Phosphorus/Manganese
Heart	—Potassium
Kidneys	—Chlorine
Nails/Hair	—Silicon
Skin/Circulation	—Sulphur/Silicon/Oxygen
Spleen	—Chlorine/Copper
Teeth/Bones	—Fluorine/Calcium
Adrenals	—Trace of Zinc
Liver	—Sulphur/Iron
Pituitary Gland	—Bromine
Stomach/Digestive System	—Chlorine/Sodium
Tissues/Secretions	—Potassium/Chlorine
Lungs/Respiratory System	—Oxygen/Iron

If you decide you want to take supplements, a qualified health practitioner needs to be consulted to advise on the correct amount of minerals needed.

Grains

Wheat, barley, rice, millet, buckwheat, oats and corn are all extremely important in a well-balanced diet. When prepared properly, they satisfy hunger and taste good. They provide energy and endurance and when combined with legumes and vegetables, supply all the elements of nutrition necessary for human development. Grains must be chewed properly to incorporate saliva, which is needed to start the digestion process. Soaking in cold water for several hours or overnight if possible, helps to release the nutrients that make grains more easily digested. Do not cook them in the soak water. For those who have poor digestion or are ill, cook the grain in plenty of fresh water till very soft, almost to gruel consistency. This way you gain most benefit from the grain. Puffed grains and commercial cereals are highly processed, so limit their use.

Barley

Barley is considered to be the most acid-forming grain but it has so many other good properties that it is recommended. Whole or sproutable barley contains more fibre, twice the calcium, three times the iron and 25% more protein than pearl barley. Barley is good for the nerves and muscles and it is well worth using whole barley although it does take a little longer to cook. Soaking barley beforehand speeds up cooking time. Cook in the ratio of one cup of barley to four cups of water, for one hour. Soup made with barley and green kale is good for increasing calcium intake.

Bran

Bran is good for red blood cell formation, but can cause constipation if not enough liquid is absorbed during digestion.

Corn

Corn, also called maize, is the most commonly used grain in many countries and fresh corn on the cob has many enzymes and vitamins. It is best not to cook it for more than a few minutes because cooking makes corn a much more starchy vegetable and it is harder to digest. Corn does not contain niacin and should not form the larger part of a diet. It is best in a mixed diet with vegetables.

Millet

Millet is an alkaline-forming grain which cooks quite quickly. Use hulled millet, otherwise you won't be able to cook it soft enough to eat. Millet has a high amino acid and silicon content and can be used frequently by those with celiac problems. Cook one cup of millet to three cups of water for about 30 minutes, after which it can be used in the same way as other grains.

Millet is a non-acid grain and does not leach calcium from the tissues. When cooked, millet releases a bland, soothing mucilaginous substance which acts as an intestinal lubricant aiding elimination. Millet is unique among the grains in that it contains all essential amino acids and is a complete protein. It is also high in lecithin, an essential nerve requirement.

Oats

Oats are rich in silicon and renew bones and connective tissue. They also contain the phosphorous needed by brain and nerve tissues and strengthen cardiac muscles. Oats are generally thought of in the form of breakfast porridge but they can be used in soups, puddings, breads and savoury loaves. For porridge, cook one cup of rolled oats to five cups of water. Stir occasionally until boiling and simmer for 10–15 minutes, stirring occasionally. The longer they cook, the better oats are digested and supply nutrients.

Rice

Whole brown rice contains a large amount of B vitamins, bran and fibre, as well as the rice germ and its essential oils. It is also very easy to digest if cooked and chewed properly, and can be eaten by those who have allergies to gluten. Made into a gruel, rice is very useful when one is very weak and unable to digest most other foods. Rice can have almost any other food added to it, savoury or sweet and short-grain brown rice is the easiest to use. Rices other than brown rice have been treated and have lost much of their nutrient value. Wild rice is not a true rice, it is more in the corn family, but makes a nice change for pilaf and rice salads. Brown rice can be cooked by several methods. The most common is to add one cup of brown rice to three cups of water, cover and bring to the boil, simmering until the rice is soft, and then rinse. According to where the rice was grown (some rice is harder and drier), cook for half to three quarters of an hour, then rinse under running hot or cold water, depending on how the rice is to be used.

Spelt

Spelt is a relative of wheat and has not been used very much until recently. It has mostly been fed to racehorses and cattle as a replacement for oats but has now been rediscovered as a beneficial food for humans. Although coming from the wheat family, spelt can generally be tolerated by those allergic to wheat. Spelt has a hearty flavour that is lacking in some other grains. Spelt is higher in protein and fat than wheat and its fibre content is water soluble, allowing for better nutrient assimilation by the body. Spelt is a good grain for those with digestive problems. It comes in the form of whole grain, pastas, flours, cereal and breads. As the grain has a very thick husk, spelt is not usually treated with pesticides or other chemicals.

Wheat

Wheat, eaten in small quantities, is one of the most useful grains as it absorbs a wider range of minerals from the soil than other grains. Unfortunately, most wheat is over-refined and has been genetically altered to resist diseases, which partly explains why some people are allergic to it. We are constantly exposed to rancid and over-refined wheat products in the production of foods. When grains are milled, their oil is exposed to the air and considered rancid.

Pastas

There is a large variety of pastas on the market, made from almost every grain. Those made from wheat are the most acid-forming, so try using the other grain pastas as wheat is included in many other foods. Care needs to be taken with the cooking of rice and buckwheat pastas as it is easy to overcook them. A good rule of thumb for most pastas is to cook them *al dente* in plenty of boiling water. Drain and rinse under cold running water and plunge back into a pot of fresh boiling water for 30 seconds just before serving. Pastas are a carbohydrate food and if the body is required to cope with more than it needs, the excess will be stored as fat. Pasta once a week is enough.

Healing properties of grains:
Amaranth—large amounts of protein and calcium lysine
Barley—soothes inflammations, reduces tumours, edema
Buckwheat—rutin, antidote agent, x-rays, radiation and blood pressure
Corn/Polenta—nourishes the heart and improves appetite
Millet—alkalising, benefits stomach and spleen, balances acidity
Oats—strengthens nerves, spleen/pancreas, heart muscles and removes cholesterol

Quinoa—strengthens kidneys, has more calcium than milk. Also has iron and vitamins

Rye—strengthens liver, gall bladder, cleans liver and arteries

Wheat—strengthens heart muscle, is not good for those with tumours and growths

Spelt—strengthens spleen/pancreas, balances and treats diarrhoea and constipation

Kamut—non-allergenic, rich in unsaturated fats and protein

Noodles—made from the above grains contain large amounts of phytic acid which binds minerals in the body causing the minerals already in the body to be inaccessible to the system. This leaves rice noodles as the best of this type of product.

Congee

Is a very thin porridge made from half a cup of rice and three cups of water. Cook the rice in the water in a covered saucepan or crock pot for at least four hours. Use a very low heat underneath a pan. The longer it cooks the more nutritious it becomes. Other ingredients can be added for different symptoms but the basic congee is very alkalising.

Congees—alkalising, nutritious and replenishes the blood. Harmonises the digestion and can be tolerated well by the very ill person. Foods to add to a congee for a more effective meal are:

Adzuki Beans—diuretic, helps relieve gout and edema

Carrot—digestive and eliminates flatulence

Celery—benefits large intestine

Fennel—settles stomach, expels gas and cures hernia

Ginger—antiseptic, helps indigestion, diarrhoea and vomiting

Leek—good for chronic diarrhoea

Radish—digestive, benefits the diaphragm area

Brown Rice—diuretic, thirst quenching and nourishing

Yoghurt and Honey—beneficial to heart and lungs.

Legumes

Beans, peas and lentils are an important source of protein and are good for the kidneys. They are often avoided because of problems with flatulence and allergies. These problems may be due to improper preparation and cooking or poor combinations (wrong choices of legume). Legumes such as great northern, navy, fava, lima, mung beans and chickpeas (garbanzo) should be soaked in cold water overnight if possible.

Legumes are time-consuming but worth the trouble. Preparation and cooking can be a mystery, but once you get into the routine of using this very important food you will be amazed at the variety you can achieve in your meals.

Soaking promotes digestibility, faster cooking and allows more minerals to be accessed. Soaking also starts the sprouting process and eliminates phytic acid. Always cook beans separately, and then add to other dishes.

- Soak them overnight, with a strip of kombu (seaweed) in cold water.
- Cover them well with water because beans are very absorbent.
- Pour off soaking water when ready to cook (gas-producing enzymes are released into the soak water).
- Add fresh water, adding back the kombu and bring to the boil.
- Pour off this water, add more fresh water (and the kombu) and cook till tender—varies from ½ to 1 hour.
- Add 1 teaspoon cumin or fennel for each cup of beans, if desired.
- Add a little tamari, miso, cider vinegar or sea salt when beans are almost cooked, if desired.
- Rinse beans well and use hot or cold with many varieties of dressing, or add them to soups/casseroles.

Lentils

Lentils do not require much preparation. It is generally not necessary to soak them, but this does improve their digestibility. If you decide not to soak them, wash well, removing all small stones or other foreign objects (often they have quite a lot). Cook in plenty of water, although they do not expand as much as legumes and only take about 20 to 30 minutes to cook. Lentils can be cooked with other foods in the same pot.

Sprouting Grains and Seeds

Grains and seeds are at their greatest stage of vitality when sprouted. They then have a dramatic increase in vitamin and enzyme content. Protein is turned into amino acids and crude fat is broken down into free fatty acids, making the nutrients easier to digest and assimilate. Most sprouts that come from large grains are better cooked lightly. You can sprout alfalfa, lentils, mung beans, sunflower, wheat and rye. To sprout:

- Soak 2 tablespoons of seeds in cold water for at least 12 hours in a wide-mouthed jar (covering mouth of jar with muslin or sprouting screen and secure with rubber band)
- Drain and stand upright so excess water drains away
- Rinse twice daily until sprouts are ready. Best eaten when there are two small leaves showing.

Alfalfa sprouts: this tiny plant, when grown in soil, can produce roots up to 30 metres long, thus reaching many minerals and nutrients not reached by other plants. Alfalfa sprouts clean the intestines and take harmful acids out of the blood. They contain ample protein, carotene (equal to carrots), calcium, iron and magnesium, which is why they are recommended in healthy diets.

Healing properties of legumes

Adzuki Beans—benefit the heart and small intestine, kidney and reduces swelling

Black Bean—diuretic, benefits kidneys

Great Northern and Navy Bean—benefits lungs

Kidney Bean—diuretic, treats swellings and edema

Lima Bean—highly alkalising, benefits liver and lungs

Garbanzo/Chickpeas—contains iron and benefits stomach, pancreas and heart

Lentil—benefits heart, circulation, adrenal system

Mung Bean—benefits liver and gall bladder, treats high blood pressure, acidosis and food poisoning

Soy Bean—very difficult to digest in their whole form, nutritious when made into milk, tofu, tempeh, soy bean sprouts; removes food stagnation and arthritis.

Seasonings that help with digestion of legumes are:

Coriander, cumin and ginger (lentil, mung, adzuki)

Sage, thyme and oregano (lentil and kidney)

Dill and basil (lentil, chickpeas, split peas)

Fennel and cumin (kidney)

Mint and garlic (chickpea and lentil).

Nuts and Seeds

Nuts and seeds become rancid and lose their nutrients when they are hulled and shelled. They still continue to deteriorate even when vacuum-packed without oxygen. Rancidity can cause irritation to lining of stomach and intestines.

The pancreatic enzymes needed to digest the oils and fats in these nuts are thereby retarded. There is evidence to suggest that vitamins A, E and F in the body can be destroyed by eating rancid nuts and seeds. They can also upset the gall bladder and liver. It is best if you want to eat nuts and seeds, to buy them still in their shell. The oil in these products can combine with plastic to form plasticises. Also buy and eat organically grown seeds and nuts as any poisons used in their growing accumulate in the seeds of all plants.

Well-grown nuts and seeds can contribute protein to the diet but need to be eaten in moderation as they can be very heavy in the stomach. Almonds are one of the most balanced and nutritious of nuts and should be bought with their brown skin still on. This protects the oil in them from oxidising. There are benefits in eating the brown skin and it is possible to make them more digestible by soaking for six to 12 hours in water. The almond is alkalising and all other nuts are acidifying.

Seaweeds

The powers of sea vegetables have been known for centuries. Sea plants contain 10 to 20 times the minerals of land plants, and an abundance of vitamins and other properties essential to man. Certain sea vegetables actually remove radioactive and toxic metal wastes from our bodies. They can remove phlegm and clean the lymphatic system. They alkalise the blood, lower cholesterol and fat in the blood, and are beneficial to the thyroid gland. They are excellent sources of calcium, amino acids and iron, varying from 10 times to 3,000 times, depending on the type of sea vegetable. Until recently, seaweeds were classed as pollution-free because they were generally harvested from pollution-free deep water and they also had the ability to reject toxins, which is part of their incredible usefulness. Nowadays, because of all the toxins dumped into sea water, the pollution-free claim is not able to be made.

Agar Agar (also sold as Kanten in flakes or powder)

A vegetable gelatin, agar agar does not need refrigeration to set to a firm jelly. It promotes digestion and contains no calories, but has most of the properties of other seaweeds. To use agar agar, add one dessertspoon to a cup of hot liquid, stir and simmer until dissolved. Add to juice to make a jelly or to cooked vegetables to make a terrine or aspic-based mould.

Agar Agar benefits the lungs and heart. It reduces swellings and inflammation. It also promotes digestion and weight loss. Agar Agar carries radioactive and toxic wastes from the body and is a good source of calcium and iron.

Hijike and Arame

Hijike and arame are thread-like lengths of seaweed containing good quantities of vitamin B2 and niacin. As with other seaweeds, they support hormone function. Soak for 30 minutes in warm water and chop. There is no need to cook them. Add to any grain, soup, bread, salad, tofu or vegetable dish.

Hijike is a diuretic and reduces phlegm. It benefits the thyroid and contains calcium, iron and iodine. It helps normalise blood sugar levels and contains valuable quantities of B2 and Niacin. It supports the hormone functions.

Arame benefits the thyroid and softens hardened areas and masses in the body. High in iodine and calcium it alleviates high blood pressure and builds bones and teeth. Traditionally used to treat feminine problems.

Kombu and Kelp

Kombu and kelp greatly increase the nutritional value of any food prepared using them as they are considered the most completely mineralised of foods. Kelp is available in powder or tablet form. It can be used in a salt shaker on the table and, because of its salty flavour, can replace the need for salt in foods.

Kombu and kelp are excellent added to dried beans during cooking, the minerals help to balance the protein and oils and they increase the digestibility of beans by breaking down the tough fibres. Break or cut the kombu with scissors and add with other ingredients to soup or bean dishes. If using in salads, cook for one hour first.

Kombu is a member of the kelp family and is the largest and longest of all sea plants growing up to 500 meters. As well as all the properties of the sea plants it benefits the kidneys and is anticoagulant. It relieves hormone imbalance and is a natural fungicide. It increases the depth of the breath and restores tired muscles and removes fungal and Candida overgrowths. It relieves coughing and reduces tumors.

Both kombu and kelp are excellent added to beans as the minerals help to balance the protein and oils in them, adding to their digestibility. Use sparingly during pregnancy or if dealing with constant diarrhoea.

Nori

The fibres of nori are more tender than other sea plants, so more easily digested. Nori has the highest protein content of sea plants and is rich in Vitamins A, B and niacin. It helps decrease cholesterol and useful to alleviate pain, goiter, edema, high blood pressure, warts and rickets. It helps the digestion of fatty foods.

Nori is well-known as the wrapping of rice to make sushi. It can be used in many ways. The only thing you can't do with nori is cook it in a liquid. It disintegrates into quite a messy green froth. Nori, if not eaten as sushi or in similar recipes, can be cut up and sprinkled on any food. It can even be used as a pie base or cut in smaller pieces and brushed with a water-damped pastry brush and fitted into muffin tins, then filled with your favorite mix and re-warmed in the oven.

Wakame

One of the seaweeds higher in calcium (hijiki is the highest). It is rich in niacin and thiamin promoting healthy hair and skin and purifies the blood. Like kombu, it softens tough fibres of foods it is cooked with.

Points to know when adding sea vegetables to your diet

With the exception of nori, it is a good idea to rinse the sea vegetables of any salt residue before you use them. It will take about a week of use to accustomise your digestive system and taste buds to dealing effectively with sea vegetables.

Fresh sea vegetables harvested from the sea or beaches can be washed well and stored in a fridge or dried in a dark place with good air flow and then stored in dark glass. They will keep for a long time if dried well. With the exception of nori, all dried sea vegetables require soaking in cold water before use. Kombu and wakame need boiling in a liquid and hijiki and arame can be used after soaking. Agar Agar needs to be stirred into a liquid and then simmered and stirred until it dissolves. One teaspoon to one cup of liquid for jam.

Eggs

While eggs are classed as a good protein source with eight amino acids, they can also be one of the most common allergenic foods. They are best kept very cool and all products using eggs should be cooked thoroughly as salmonella can penetrate the porous eggshell and thus make uncooked eggs quite dangerous. Chickens enclosed in poultry farms are devoid of almost all nutrients. So check the labelling on egg containers as they can be misleading. Compare free-range eggs purchased from a health food store with eggs produced by large poultry farms.

Eggs have a number of functions in baked products and it is not possible to replace all of these with substitutes. Eggs act as a structural component and nutrient source, providing lightness, flavour and moisture. Structure is not severely affected by omitting eggs as long as a binder and sufficient liquid is added (3 tablespoons for every egg omitted).

The nutrient quality of eggs cannot be substituted and lecithin in egg yolk acts as an emulsifier for the fat in baked goods and also in the human system, helping to break down the fat particles. In egg-free recipes the fat is often melted and boiled with the liquid and quickly stirred into the dry ingredients to stop dispersion of the fat and water. The lecithin in the egg yolk breaks up the fat, so for 1 egg, alternative substitute:

- 2 tablespoons cold cooked sago (only successful for substituting up to 2 eggs)
- 2 tablespoons flour, ½ teaspoon seasoning, ½ teaspoon baking powder and 2 tablespoons liquid
- 2 tablespoons water, ½ teaspoon baking powder (good in biscuit/cake recipes requiring only 1 egg)
- 1 mashed banana in biscuits, cakes, pancakes and muffins.

Also:

- Gelatin works well in puddings and desserts: 1 tablespoon to every 2 cups liquid
- 250 grams dried apricots soaked in water for several hours or overnight. Blend, add extra water if necessary, strain and store in refrigerator. One generous tablespoon will substitute for 1 egg (freeze portions for further use)
- Ground flaxseed is a good egg substitute in biscuit, cake, pancake and muffin recipes. Add 1 cup ground flaxseed to 3 cups cold water. Bring to boil, stirring constantly. Boil for 3 minutes, cool and store in the refrigerator in a closed jar. 1 tablespoon will substitute for 1 egg
- Replace egg as the binder in meat loaf or rissoles with 1 cup puffed rice to each 500 grams mince
- Use tapioca or arrowroot flour as binders. Instead of using 2 cups rice flour, use 1½ cups flour and ½ cup tapioca arrowroot plus 1 tablespoon of extra liquid.

Sweeteners

Sugar

Sugar is a major force in our bodies and we need it, but in the right form. The sugars in whole foods are balanced with the proper minerals and the energy obtained from the breaking down of these sugars is enduring. The highs and lows we experience from taking in refined sugars (hidden in so many processed foods) cause, among many other conditions, an acid effect in the body, an upset mineral balance, and lowering of the immune system. This leads to a blood sugar imbalance and more sugar cravings, as well as an increase in the craving for meat and other high-protein foods. Grains and vegetables chewed very well will gradually reduce the cravings for sweetness from the wrong sources.

Honey

In small quantities, honey can be substituted for sugar, but honey is highly refined by bees and has more calories than white sugar. Raw, cold extracted honey does contain some minerals and enzymes and does not upset the body's mineral balance. When heated, honey loses its nutrient value.

Grain Malts

Made from fermented rice or barley, grain malts are only one-third as sweet as sugar yet contain complex sugars and many of the nutrients in grains. They take longer to digest so they don't produce the highs and lows that one can experience when eating cane sugar.

Stevia Powder or Liquid

Becoming better known, stevia is a small herb that is native to Latin America and the southern United States. The leaves and flowers of this plant are 30 times sweeter than sugar, and stevia can be used without ill effect by diabetics. Stevia does not work as well as other sweeteners in baked goods because it doesn't have the moistening effect of cane sugar.

Fruit Concentrates

Fruit concentrates are another source of sweetening, but because of their concentrated nature, their sugar content becomes very high. Fruit concentrates are far from being whole unprocessed foods. Dried fruits which have been soaked well in water can be pureed and used as sweeteners.

Cane Sugar Substitutes

Not all recipes will work with sugar substitutes. One cup of white sugar is equivalent to:

- ¾ cup pure maple syrup—reduce total liquids by 2 tablespoons
- ½ cup honey—reduce total liquids by ¼ cup
- 1 cup molasses—reduce liquids by ½ cup
- 1½ cup sorghum—reduce total liquids by ¼ cup

- 1 cup pure corn syrup—reduce total liquids by ¼ cup
- When using substitutes, prevent burning by lowering the baking temperature by 20°C (40°F)
- To measure liquid sweeteners, first moisten cup with hot water
- Use unsweetened fruit juice in place of other liquid
- Fructose (fruit sugar) can be used to replace sugar in cereals, drinks and desserts (be careful that you are not allergic to the source from which the sugar is derived)
- When substituting glucose or dextrose for sugar, remember they are usually derived from corn
- In baking, use dried fruits to add sweetness.

Carob

The carob tree is one of the oldest known fruit-bearing trees. It originated in the Mediterranean region and was known as St John's bread.

- Carob flour and powder supply protein, carbohydrates, minerals, calcium and phosphorous.
- Carob powder has a very low fat content.
- Carob can be used as a substitute for chocolate or coffee in cooked products and in hot or cold drinks.
- 1 square of cooking chocolate is equivalent to 1 tablespoon of carob powder (when using carob powder use a little less sweetening than the recipe calls for, as carob is a natural sweetener).
- Carob needs no added sweeteners.
- Carob is an alkaline-forming food and does not contain caffeine.
- Carob chocolate usually contains coconut or palm oil fats (saturated fat).

Dairy Products

Butter

Although butter is a saturated fat, it is a better choice for a spread than the chemically produced margarine. Butter goes through three almost natural processes in its production. Clarified butter (ghee) is actually of benefit to our system because the process of clarifying produces butyric acid, a mono-unsaturated oil that protects the heart. To make a quite healthy spread, mix softened butter with half the volume of olive oil (2:1) and refrigerate. To keep it firm at room temperature add the same quantity of lecithin granules as oil to the mixture (2:1:1).

Cheese

Cheese in all forms is a saturated fat and best used sparingly. The cheesemaking process makes it harder for our system to access the nutrients that are available from whole unadulterated milk.

Seed Cheese

Seed cheese is high in vitamins and enzymes and is easy to make and digest. You can add herbs, onion, garlic and any savoury seasoning you like. It is great spread on crackers or when used to stuff small tomatoes, mushrooms etc. You will need ½ cup sunflower seeds, or almonds or cashews, and 1 cup of filtered water.

Method:

Put the seeds or nuts in a glass jar, cover with filtered water and let them soak overnight. Drain and rinse. Place seeds and 1 cup of filtered water in a blender and run blender until mixture is creamy. Return mixture to the jar and let it sit in a warm place or in a pan of hot water for 5 to 9 hours or until it separates (into curds and whey). Take the soft cheese part off the top and refrigerate or place the mixture in a cheesecloth and squeeze tightly, letting this 'bag' hang over a bowl for a day, making for a firmer cheese.

FISH

Fish is a better source of protein than meat. Fish also has the decided advantage of supplying omega 3, an essential fatty acid that, among many other uses, keeps the blood viscosity at a level where it doesn't form clots. Deep-sea fish are the most beneficial as they supply a good quantity of cobalt, iodine and fluorine, as well as the omegas. 200–300 grams of fish each week is sufficient to supply the body's needs of these and many other nutrients. Shellfish can be full of toxins and low in fatty acids, so keep them to a minimum.

BREADS

It is worth making your own bread, as many of the so-called wholesome and healthy wholewheat loaves available in the stores are neither. Often, the flour used is mixed wholewheat and processed white; so much of the fibre is lost. Even the distinctive brown colouring may come from caramel. Many such loaves often have as many additives as white bread and are manufactured in much the same way.

When making bread use small amounts of sea salt; sweeteners and oils are not necessary. Make bread in the morning and bake bread at night. On warm sunny days it rises better. Make bread when you feel vital and happy. Your energy will ensure a better loaf (macrobiotic principle).

Breadmaking machines are very useful. In a good nutritional diet you can use fresh milled flour which retains all the grain nutrients. There is no need to use chemical additives to keep it fresh and you can avoid baker's yeast and use a sourdough culture.

Flours

• Barley flour makes a sticky bread and can be combined 50:50 with wholewheat flour for lightness.

• Brown rice yields a sweeter and smoother bread. Use 20% in combination with other flours.

- Buckwheat makes a good dark, heavy winter bread. Use in combination with wheat and rice flours.
- Chestnut flour gives a light bread. Good combined with small amounts of other flours.
- Cornmeal flour gives a good light bread. Best combined with small amounts of other flours.
- Garbanzo (chickpea) flour can be used alone or mixed with other flours, especially good in sauces and pancakes.
- Kamut flour is light in texture and can be substituted in equal amount for wholewheat pastry flour in cake, pie and muffin recipes.
- Millet flour: always combine with other flour, especially wholewheat (one third millet/two thirds wholewheat).
- Oat flour is light in texture and can be substituted for pastry flour. It adds moistness to cakes and pastries. Add approximately 20% to corn, wholewheat or rice flours.
- Rye flour makes a sticky bread and can be combined 50:50 with rice or wholewheat flour for a lighter bread. 100% rye bread greatly improves in flavour after several days.
- Soy flour, add small amounts to other flours for a smoother and moister texture.
- Spelt flour can be substituted 100% for wheat in bread recipes. Usually well-tolerated by those allergic to wheat.

SOY PRODUCTS

Miso

Is a fermented paste made from soy beans and grains. There are three basic types of miso:
- soybean (*hatcho*)
- barley (*mugi*)
- rice (*kome*)

as well as many variations.

Miso contains amino acids, protein, traces of vitamin B12 and is a live food containing lactobacillus bacteria. It creates an alkaline condition in the body that promotes resistance to disease.

Most of the nutrients in miso are destroyed by boiling, so add the paste to soups and stews just before serving. A teaspoon of miso dissolved in a cup of hot water has the ability to settle an upset stomach by creating an alkaline environment. It helps too, when you have overeaten or are undergoing chemotherapy. Because it adds a hearty flavour, miso is sometimes overused by people when changing to a meatless diet. Be aware that it is stronger than meat because of its ageing process and sea salt content. When used in moderation, it provides excellent nutrition. You can add it to stews, soups, gravies, sauces, dressings, stuffings, dips and spread sparingly on toast.

Soy Beans

Soybeans are very alkalising and can be a valuable food. They help remove toxins from the body and provide phyto-oestrogens and trytophan. But soybeans are the hardest bean to digest, and unless very well cooked, inhibit digestive enzymes. The fermentation process, such as that used in the making of tempeh, tofu, miso and soy sauce, eliminates the trypsin effect of the soybean. This process also makes them easier to assimilate and so it is better to use these products than to use whole unprocessed soybeans.

Soy Milk

There are many soy milks on the market. Choose one that is made from organic whole soybeans and use it in moderation. This will provide protein and calcium and can be used in the same way as cow's milk (except for small children). There is oat milk and rice milk as well. These products are good to use as they do not cause the digestive problems that can arise from using cow's milk.

Soy Yoghurt

Soy yoghurt has many of the same nutritional properties as cow's milk yoghurt, except lacto bacillus, but has the added benefits of the soybean.

Tempeh

Originating in Indonesia, this fermented food is made from cooked soybean bound together by a mould. There are many flavours and varieties. Asian tempeh can be a good source of vitamin B12 but, when made in Western countries, the B12 content is not as high because of the clean environment of the manufacturing area, so B12 is often injected into the finished product. Tempeh must be cooked either by baking, steaming or boiling, and is improved by marinating, as is tofu.

Tofu

Tofu is a processed soybean curd that originated in China thousands of years ago, and developed to improve the digestibility of the valued soybean. Tofu contains protein, B vitamins and minerals, and a calcium content equal to that of cow's milk. We do not need a lot of tofu but it is a versatile product which can be baked, steamed, boiled, sautéed and even eaten raw (because of its blandness it soaks up whatever flavouring it is put with). To store, cover with water, keep in an airtight container/jar in a cool place and change the water daily.

Shiitake Mushrooms

This food that research scientists have suggested has marked anti-cancer effects, is effective against infections, enhances the body's immune system and gives you energy, vitality and vigor.

Lentinan (a chemical in shiitake mushrooms) is so effective that the government of Japan approved it as the first anti-cancer product possessing life prolonging effects in patients with stomach cancer.

Wayne Reilly, senior consultant at Cell Dynamics, CSIRO concurs with other world scientists and states that apart from its value as a culinary delicacy, the Shiitake mushroom is endowed with anti-carcinogenic, anti-cholesterol and immuno-stimulating properties.

The Lentinan content is not affected by cooking. Consumed in its natural form, the Shiitake mushroom tastes fabulous. It will naturally enhance the flavour of any meal. To obtain the maximum benefit of the Lentinan content of the Shiitake mushroom, it is recommended that 300 grams per week per person be included in the diet.

Fresh Shiitake mushrooms containing Lentinan (an immune-enhancing component) are now available locally grown. Shiitake mushrooms are grown on natural ingredients unlike other mushrooms which are grown on compost. This gives Shiitake mushrooms a very distinct flavour. Mushrooms are a good source of Vitamin B12, folate, potassium and dietary fibre. 100 grams of Shiitake mushrooms contains approximately 13 calories (55 kjs).

To store Shiitake mushrooms, it is recommended that they be refrigerated in a brown paper bag to prevent moisture loss. When refrigerated, Shiitake mushrooms will last approximately three weeks. However, to utilise the maximum benefit of the Lentinan content they are best consumed within seven days of purchase.

Dried Shiitake mushrooms also contain Lentinan and are much cheaper when purchased at an Asian grocery. Just soak in warm water for 20 minutes before using in the same way as fresh Shiitake mushrooms. Dried Shiitake keep for a very long time and do not lose their usefulness.

OILS AND FATS

There are three types of oil or fat:

Saturated

Solid at room temperature and primarily from animal sources, and include coconut, peanut, palm and cottonseed.

Mono-unsaturated

Olive and sesame, canola and avocado. Liquid at room temperature, solid when cold.

Polyunsaturated

Flax, soy and walnut must not be heated. Liquid at room temperature and also when cold; comes from the vegetable kingdom.

Some fat or oil is essential to the digestion of our food and it provides a satisfying effect when we eat.

Our earliest ancestors ate the meat and the fat that was naturally in that meat when it was cooked. It was a natural accompaniment. The amount of fat was in balance with the meat. The difference with today's meat is that it is not grown naturally. Cattle can be fed a combination of chemicals and what is not excreted is stored in the fat of the animal in very concentrated amounts. Added to all the other allowed chemicals in our food, it is no wonder people are getting sicker at a younger age. If you feel the need for meat, it is better to have high-quality, low-fat meat only once or twice a week—just a smallish portion to satisfy your needs. Meat has some nutrients that are not easy to obtain from other sources, B12 and iron are just two and animal phosphorus is needed in very small quantities for those who depend on a high level of right brain activity.

As protein is in good supply from other foods the needed fat is better taken from a vegetable source, like flax or olives. Flax and olive oil can be obtained cold-pressed, meaning the oil has not been extracted with heat and/or chemicals. When the oils are cold-pressed they retain all their nutrients, especially omega 3, which is essential for us. We need only a very small amount of omega 6 and 9.

If possible, buy oils in dark glass containers or light-free cans, as light causes the oil to lose most of its nutritional properties. Oils labeled cold-extracted and unrefined only retain their nutritional properties if they are used cold.

Most other oils are extracted by high heat and, as such, are useless nutrient-wise and, in some cases, quite harmfully out of balance. Flax oil should never be heated as it loses its beneficial properties (and tastes unpleasant). You can add flax oil to dressings cold, or take from a spoon, in a juice, or poured over food just before eating. If you need to cook with oil, use olive oil at a ratio of 50:50 with water to sauté vegetables or pan-fry foods, as the water stops the oil heating to the carcinogenic point.

Use olive oil to grease a cooking pan as oil sprays are loaded with chemicals. Cakes and desserts can be made without fat of any kind, they are just a little drier in texture and don't keep in an edible state for very long.

The right types of fat, or fatty acids more correctly, are necessary in our diet. We need a very small amount of mono-unsaturated and a slightly larger amount of polyunsaturated fat. Once converted into fatty acid, these fats and oils are used in cellular function, are involved in metabolic processes, are needed by hormones to regulate body processes, and are burned for energy.

Mono-unsaturated and polyunsaturated fats are both useful in the system and are derived from plants. The chemical action with regard to nutrition is quite difficult to understand but there are properties in both that we need in balance. Mono-unsaturated oils contain a predominance of omega 6, 9 and some 3. The most common of these are safflower, sunflower, canola and olive oil. When heated and used for cooking they should be used only once and discarded.

We can function very well without saturated fats, which are the cheapest to manufacture and are used for most deep-fried food, in bakery goods, and in many ready prepared foods in packets and jars.

BEVERAGES

Plain Water

Plain water is very necessary to life and the recommended quantity varies. We can make some of it more interesting and therapeutic by adding various herbs. There are a huge number of herb teas on the market, but you should avoid drinking one or two of them exclusively as they can have a therapeutic effect. Make sure the kinds you drink are suitable for you (check with a natural therapist before using a particular one on a regular basis and vary them for the properties they contain).

Animal Milks

Animal milks are a necessary choice in some cases and care should be taken to choose the right one. Pasteurisation (the heating of milk to high temperature and cooling rapidly), plus homogenisation (chemically dispersing fat evenly) both have a denuding effect on milk and the products produced from it. Although the original product may contain calcium, it is seriously depleted when these products are pasteurised ie. in milk, cheese, canned foods etc. it is difficult for our system to obtain any benefit from their use.

Bouillon

One teaspoon of mineral bouillon in a cup of hot water is a tasty hot drink instead of soup.

Buttermilk

Buttermilk is good as a laxative.

Coconut Milk

Made from the flesh of the coconut is quite nutritious but a high-fat food so needs to be used sparingly.

Goat's Milk

Fresh or in dried whey, supplies potassium, sodium phosphate and calcium and is easier for most systems to assimilate as it has a smaller fat curd and can be digested better than treated cow's milk.

Grain and Nut Milk

Very nutritious and suitable to be used in smoothies and desserts. Nut milk was made and used centuries ago. Europeans made almond and walnut milk, Arabs made almond milk, Indians made coconut milk and the Chinese made a soybean milk. Native Americans made milk from pecan and hickory nuts.

Soy Milk

Research shows that although some soy milk is fortified with calcium, the system only absorbs about 75% of that calcium. Soy milk is a good source of protein, B vitamins and iron and is free of lactose.

If drinking, it is best used when diluted 2:1 with water, as soy milk is quite 'heavy' and contains fairly high quantities of protein, which can be hard on digestion processes (possibly dehydrating, as protein requires liquid to digest).

SEASONINGS

Liquid bouillons and dried organic vegetable powders can provide added flavour in your soups, sauces and casseroles. Miso, tamari and soy are useful, as are fresh herbs and spices. Natural yeast powders can also help with flavour while adding extra nutrients. These seasonings are a better choice to use in your food as most of the generally used ones are chemically formulated.

Tamari

A naturally made and aged soy sauce, twice as strong as commercially made soy sauce—nutritious as it is made from soy beans and is wheat free.

Herbamare

A powdered organic vegetables and herb seasoning which can be sprinkled on food and used in cooking. Use sparingly as it contains salt.

Sea Salt

Natural organic sea salt contains many essential minerals and must be used sparingly in cooking and not sprinkled on food.

Braggs Bouillon

A soy based, brown strong liquid especially suited to flavouring soups, sauces and casseroles. Nutritious and pleasant-tasting as a hot drink.

Turmeric

Turmeric contains curcumin which has several cancer-retarding properties. Curcumin suppresses the nuclear growth factor kappa beta (NF-KB) which tends to fuel malignant cell proliferation and inhibits cell growth at the G2 stage. Curcumin also blocks cancer promoting chemicals such as xeno-oestrogens and nitrosamines. It protects against oxidative damage to cell DNA by radiation. It induces more normal cell apoptosis (self-destruction) mechanisms that malignant cells tend to lack. It inhibits angiogenesis necessary for tumour growth and enhances cell immunity.

Absorption of curcumin is dramatically enhanced by piperine added to capsules of curcumin.

Tomatoes contain lycopene, onions contain quercetin and garlic contains allicin. The bio-availability of these is enhanced by lightly cooking in cold-pressed extra virgin olive oil.

VEGETABLES

Vegetables are vital in our diet and ideally should be organically grown, and for complete nutrition, eaten with a grain. Also, eating those vegetables that are in season and grown in the area you live in are the best for your body.

Vegetables are generally cleansing for the body and purify the blood while grains build the body. Also your body benefits if it doesn't have to deal with too much of a mixture of food in any one meal. For example try to use no more than four to five vegetables or other foods in any meal. You will obtain better assimilation and nutrition from those foods when they are better digested.

Lightly cooked vegetables retain most of their vitamins and minerals, while long, slow cooking is necessary for some of the root vegetables and are better digested by those with compromised digestive systems.

We have so many foods from all over the world and we tend to choose too much of a mixture for our body to deal with at any one time. Our body behaves better if we can eat according to our genetic background ie. not French food for breakfast, Italian for lunch and Chinese for dinner followed by a Western or English dessert. Also our system tries to deal with many of the 60,000 chemical additions used in the growing, processing and packaging of our food. Is it any wonder our bodies are complaining?

Asparagus
● supplies iodine, chlorine, sulphur, vitamin E, potassium and phosphorous
● a good tonic for the kidneys
● break off and discard the tough stem and boil or steam the rest for 7–8 minutes to remove a slightly toxic chemical

Beetroot
● supplies magnesium, potassium, manganese and sodium
● good for liver ailments, improves circulation and purifies the blood
● beetroot is an 'eliminating' food
● organic tastes better
● boil whole and serve hot or cold or to serve raw, scrub and grate, adding a little dressing.

Broccoli
● supplies calcium, phosphorous, magnesium, iron, sulphur, vitamins A and B5, and more vitamin C than citrus
● if cooked lightly will retain all its chlorophyll content which reduces its gas-forming properties.

Brussel Sprouts
● supply sulphur, potassium, phosphorous and many vitamins and minerals
● high fibre content, helps the bowels to work well
● contains sulfurophane, which helps the body to fight carcinogens
● although they look and taste like little cabbages, they are far more valuable.

Cabbage
● supplies chlorine, sulphur, chlorophyll, iodine, calcium, vitamin E and more vitamin C than citrus
● benefits all stomach problems

- 40% more calcium in green cabbage than white cabbage
- purifies the blood and deters constipation.

Capsicum
- supplies iodine, bioflavonoids and vitamin C.

Carrots
- supply calcium, phosphorous, magnesium, chlorine and vitamin A
- alkaline forming, which helps to clear acidic blood conditions
- one of the richest sources of vitamin A, an anti-oxidant that protects against cancer
- stimulates the release of wastes and clears intestinal tract
- dissolves tumours and growths.

Cauliflower
- supplies potassium, biotin, iron, and vitamin C
- contains large quantities of sulfuraphane
- high fibre content
- helps keep the body fluids balanced
- helps the heart function and maintains blood pressure.

Celery
- supplies chlorine, insulin, chlorophyll and magnesium
- reduces acids and adds essential sodium (as distinct from salt)
- improves digestion and liver function

- high in silicon (helps to renew bones, arteries and all connective tissue)
- a few stalks eaten raw will satisfy salt cravings
- helps to reduce high blood pressure.

Corn
- supplies chlorine, calcium, phosphorous, manganese and folic acid
- starch in yellow sweet corn is very easy to digest
- has one of the best fibres for our bowel
- a great bone and muscle builder
- soup made from barley and corn is very high in magnesium and is excellent for the nervous system and brain.

Cucumber
- supplies sodium, silica, chlorine and bromine
- counteracts toxins and cleanses the blood
- reduces acids and adds sodium
- acts as a digestive aid and cools the system in summer
- juice is good for kidney and bladder problems
- contains an enzyme—erepsis—that breaks down protein and cleanses the intestines
- can be used raw or cooked.

Eggplant
- one cup of steamed eggplant supplies 31 mg of iron, equal to 1 kg of beef or 10 hamburgers
- is full of vitamins and minerals.

Edible Flowers
- apple or any fruit flower, borage, clover, lavender, marigold, rose, rosemary, violet, zucchini and hibiscus.

Garlic
- supplies sulphur
- very useful for promoting circulation
- eliminates unfavourable bacteria and yeasts
- improves healthy bacteria in the intestines and eliminates many toxins from the body
- eats cholesterol on artery walls (see also onions).

Green String Beans
- supply phosphorous, manganese and nitrogen
- good nerve and body builder
- help with diabetes.

Lettuce
- supplies silicon, iron, copper, chlorophyll, biotin, potassium and chlorine
- green leafy lettuce is much richer in nutrients than head lettuce
- contains chlorophyll (plus iron, vitamins A and C) in the outer green leaves only
- try not to use hydroponically grown lettuce (or other produce grown this way) as the chemicals used to grow them are concentrated in the recycled water. Even if it is a natural fertiliser, it can become too concentrated.

Mushrooms
- supply selenium, bromine and silica
- contain antibiotic properties
- increase immunity against disease
- increase the appetite while decreasing fat levels in the blood
- reduce mucus in the respiratory tract.

Olives
- supply sodium, calcium and phosphorous
- black olives supply the highest source of potassium (rinse off brine)
- good brain and nerve food.

Onions
- supply potassium, phosphorous, iodine and silicon
- rich in sulphur, which purifies the body and cleans the arteries
- help remove heavy metals from the body
- help to keep the blood at a viscous level and avoid clotting (see also garlic).

Parsnips
- supply potassium, phosphorous, choline and sulphur
- good for spleen and pancreas
- help avoid blood clotting
- benefit the stomach, liver and gall bladder
- best used cooked in soups and stews or dry-baked in the oven.

Parsley
- supplies vitamins A and C, calcium, potassium, iron, chlorophyll, sodium and magnesium
- improves digestion
- useful in treatment of ear infection
- strengthens adrenals
- good for brain and optic nerve
- effective in treatment of kidney and urinary difficulties.

Note: not to be used by nursing mothers as it can dry up milk.

Peas
- supply phosphorous, potassium, iron and manganese
- good source of vitamin E (not frozen peas)
- good for bone formation and healthy nerves
- help kidney function.

Potatoes
- supply potassium, magnesium, sulphur, iodine, chlorine
- cook with skin on to retain their essential nutrients.

Pumpkin
- supplies silicon, potassium and iron
- helps regulate blood sugar levels
- can help bronchial problems
- use cooked: boil, bake, steam, mash or use in casseroles and stews.

Radishes
- supply potassium and choline
- good for detoxing the body

- reduce mucus and help reduce viral infection.

Spinach/Silver beet
- supply iron and chlorophyll
- useful source of vitamin A
- wash carefully and steam or boil
- very small amounts should be eaten raw as they contain oxalic acid which is reduced a little by cooking.

Sweet Potato/Yams
- supply vitamin A
- remove toxins from the body
- good mixed with pumpkin in a soup or sliced and baked in the oven.

Tomatoes
- supplies chlorine, sulphur, potassium, sodium and lycopene
- fresh tomato can help to cleanse the body
- stimulate production of gastric juices for protein digestion.

FRUIT

We are conditioned from an early age to eat lots of fruit. Much of the fruit that we eat is picked before it is properly ripe and it does not develop the expected nutrients until the sun actually ripens it. When ripening or getting soft unnaturally, it contains a lot of sugar which is destructive to the immune system and as such the fruit is not as nutritious as it should be. Buy organic fruit for the best nutritional value.

Drinking a lot of sweet fruit juice can be very weakening and can promote the growth of yeasts in the body. Fruit is generally considered not to mix well with other food during digestion as fruit digests faster and starts to ferment in the stomach while waiting for the rest of the food to be processed.

It is better to have a fruit meal on an empty stomach, ie. breakfast or mid-afternoon. Eat whole fruits rather than juices. Fruit juices should not be drunk with a meal.

Apples
- supply vitamins A, C and E, biotin and folic acid when eating the whole fruit
- one of the most useful fruits, apples contain pectin and help to clear cholesterol
- the malic acid clears harmful bacteria in the digestive tract
- the fruit and juice are beneficial for the liver and gall bladder.

Apricots
- supply vitamins A, phosphorous, iron and manganese
- useful for those with anemia
- help with lung problems such as asthma
- high in cobalt and copper
- limit apricots if you tend to have trouble with diarrhoea.

Avocadoes
- supply biotin, folic acid, calcium, potassium, sodium and magnesium
- natural source of lecithin and mono-saturated fats/oils
- a good protein
- rich in copper, which helps build red blood cells.

Bananas
- supply manganese, potassium, iron, copper, biotin and magnesium
- good for reducing blood pressure because of high potassium content
- treat hypertension
- steamed bananas are good for reducing diarrhoea, colitis and haemorrhoids
- calm the body system for cellular electrolyte balance
- very sweet, making a great sugar substitute when used as a puree.

Cherries
- supply copper and manganese
- high in easily assimilated iron
- good for gout and arthritis as they help eliminate excess body acid
- try to obtain organic cherries as most commercially grown ones are very heavily sprayed.

Figs
- supply iron, calcium and potassium
- a very alkalising fruit, can help balance acid conditions resulting from a diet high in meat and refined foods
- good for cleansing the bowel (constipation).

Grapefruit
- supply biotin, phosphorous, potassium and magnesium
- similar properties to lemons but not as useful as lemons.

Grapes
- supply manganese, silicon and folic acid
- red grapes in particular, are good blood builders
- improve the cleansing function of our glands
- help with liver problems such as hepatitis and jaundice
- the juice improves kidney function.

Lemons
- supply phosphorous, sodium and calcium
- all citrus fruits have a small amount of vitamin C
- help with digestion and are particularly cleansing
- clean the blood and help circulation
- benefit liver and absorption of minerals
- reduce flatulence
- calm the nerves
- a little juice in water first thing in the morning helps to destroy bad bacteria in the mouth and intestines and encourages the production of bile by improving liver function.

Oranges
- supply calcium, phosphorous and magnesium

- best eaten as a whole fruit and not as a juice
- usually sprayed very heavily and picked while still green
- can be quite acidic due to growing and picking procedures.

Pawpaws
- supply calcium, potassium, iron and magnesium
- particularly good for treating indigestion or if you have eaten too much protein.

Pears
- supply folic acid, silicon, potassium and iron
- beneficial for constipation problems
- help cleanse the lungs of mucus
- eat whole or have the juice first thing in the morning.

Pineapples
- supply manganese
- contain the enzyme bromelin, which can help to increase digestive ability.

Prunes
- supply iron, sodium and magnesium
- have the highest content of nerve salts (tissue salts that strengthen the nerves)
- full of minerals and help regulate acid/alkaline balance.

Raspberries
- supply iron and silicon
- thought to be beneficial in the treatment of some types of cancer.

Certain fruits contain ellagic acid, a proven inducer of apoptosis, the process by which normal, non-malignant cells exhibit a self-limited lifespan. Cancer cells grow out of control without the normal processes of limitation, as though the cell apoptosis mechanisms have been switched off.

Ellagic acid content of foods are:

- Pomegranate   15,200 mg/gr
- Raspberries   1,460
- Figs   517
- Strawberries   also quite rich
- Blueberries   also quite rich

Raspberry puree fed to experimental animals with cancer has been shown to shrink tumours. Raspberries are currently being tested in long-term clinical trials in the USA, in cancer patients and in healthy subjects (prospective studies). These trials may confirm a suspected cancer-inhibiting effect of raspberries by virtue of its content of ellagic acid.

Strawberries
- supply choline and sulphur
- rich in silicon
- good for spleen and pancreas
- eat before a meal as they can stimulate the appetite
- a good spring cleanser (helps clear the system of any accumulations of the heavier winter foods)
- organic, if possible, because they are one of the most highly sprayed fruits.

Almonds
- are a protein food
- contain a good quantity of calcium
- supply mono-unsaturated fatty acid (to keep cholesterol in check)
- more benefit is obtained from almonds if they are soaked in cold water for about 12 hours.

Peanuts
- are actually a bean, not a nut—some people are allergic to peanuts; they contain aflotoxins, a mild poison

Most other nuts have a high fat content and are best eaten straight after shelling, as the oil/fat starts to oxidise (go rancid) as soon as the air comes in contact with the unprotected oil.

FOODS AND TIPS TO BOOST THE IMMUNE SYSTEM

All grains in their natural form—not processed. The nutrients needed are contained in the outer husk or shell. Barley, rice, millet, spelt and oats.

Green Leafy Vegetables
The usefulness of these is the chlorophyll in the green part. It cleans and rebuilds blood and cells.

Sea Vegetables
Sea vegetables have lots of protein, calcium, minerals and chlorophyll. Nori, kombu and arame are some. Sushi is a good way to eat nori.

Carrots

Carrots have a nutrient called beta-carotene, or vitamin A, which blocks the production of malignant cells. Carrot juice gives a big boost to immunity. All fresh vegetable juices are useful.

Sprouts

Alfalfa, in particular, is extra-helpful to the immune system, providing many vitamins, minerals, enzymes and protein.

Broccoli, cabbage and Brussel sprouts are helpful.

Nuts and Seeds—Not Peanuts

As fresh as possible, not roasted are best. Can use nut spreads instead of butter. Definitely don't use margarine as it contains oils that are damaging to the immune system.

Fish

Add omega 3 oil to the diet. Fish is a good way to get this but there are tablets and capsules available that come from flax seed.

Shiitake Mushrooms

Dried or fresh, shiitake mushrooms contain a chemical compound called lentinan that has been proven to boost the activity of the immune system immensely.

Organic Produce

Where possible buy organic foods, particularly vegetables and fruit, so that the immune system doesn't have to deal with the possibly harmful sprays used to grow vegetables commercially.

Limit your sugar intake as sugar in all forms, even fruit, lowers the immune system. Fruit juices are very high in sugar. Fried foods put a heavy fat load into your system that makes it very hard for your cells to absorb oxygen and to rebuild effectively. Eat simple meals and get some exercise—walking is one of the best. As there are very few nutrients in processed foods, they are best avoided or at least severely limited.

DIGESTION

The following pages are an example of a simple nutritious program for two weeks. You need not follow it exactly day by day, decide how you eat each day by the way each day's food appeals to you. The main point is to keep your diet as simple as possible. Have as much as you feel like of each dish. There is no limit on quantity, better to have a bigger portion of something that appeals to you than adding another type of food—extra work for your digestion. Make sure you have your juices between meals unless you are using them instead of your meal at that time.

When you are not well, juices can supply the added cleansing and building essentials without demanding too much energy to digest. If the weather is cold, concentrate on warm food inbetween your juice. Whole meals cooked in one pot are easy and nutritious; soups, casseroles and stews with grains or pulses can supply variety and save time both in preparation and 'serving up' not to mention the washing and cleaning up. Grains and/or pulses with at least one meal a day can help to balance out that feeling of hunger. The lack of 'something' that sometimes is felt when eating a vegan type diet.

Oils combine best with non-sweet fruit and vegetables. Oil slows down digestion of proteins and starch. Green leafy vegetables aid fat and protein digestion. Dairy foods should be taken alone. Homemade yoghurt is the best choice, because it is not pasteurised after fermentation. Tomatoes eaten when they are in season are not acidifying.

If using a crock pot for slowcooking or cast-iron type casserole, these times for cooking are a general guide. One hour for large carrots, beetroot, sweet potato, turnip and pumpkin. Half an hour for yellow or green squash, artichokes, parsnips, corn on the cob, peas and beans. If vegetables are sliced thinly they are usually ready in 8 to 10 minutes.

Tree-ripened fruits can be considered to be alkaline-forming in the body and help to remove toxins from the system.

Fruits picked green and stored for long periods do not develop the necessary health-promoting properties; they instead contribute to the acidic condition of an unwell body. Avocado is best eaten with leafy green vegetables. Try not to combine it with nuts or seeds or other proteins.

Food Combining Tips for Good Digestion
Good combinations
Proteins and leafy greens
Starch and vegetables
Oil and leafy greens
Oil and acid fruits
Oil and sub-acid fruit

Poor combinations
Protein and acid fruit
Leafy greens and acid fruit
Leafy greens and sub-acid fruit

Bad combinations
Protein and starch
Oil and protein
Starch and fruit

These suggestions of food combining are the ultimate way to have your food. It can be very difficult to eat this way but it is helpful to know these combinations and to apply them, particularly when you feel unwell. See the references to what foods contain or their classification.

MONO DIET

A short period of time eating a simple diet or in fact eating only one food can sometimes be of benefit when deciding to change your diet. A quick, drastic change of your food can cause some discomfort both physically and emotionally. So if you wish to cleanse and detoxify your body, start very gently. It is also advisable to consult your health practitioner and your support people.

A good way to start is by limiting your normal food a little for a couple of days, then eating only one food for a couple of days, then slowly reintroducing other foods. If you feel better for the rest you have given your digestive system you may want to repeat the exercise by staying with one food for three to four days. The foods generally recommended are cooked brown rice and drinking only plain water or herb teas. The rice should be boiled brown rice on its own. No vegetable or seasonings.

If it is warm weather when you decide to try this cleansing diet you can use grapes or watermelon, one type of fruit only. If using grapes you can drink grape juice as well as water. Grapes are high in sugar, potassium and iron and should promote an alkaline condition. If used for a mono diet the recommend-

ation is to eat 500 grams of grapes every three to four hours for a period of one week.

Watermelon is noted for its alkaline pH and high predominance of alkaline minerals and potassium. All melons are valuable for their diuretic action on the kidneys. They combine badly with all other foods and are best eaten on an empty stomach and alone with no other food or fruit.

The length of time recommended for a mono-type diet is 10 days maximum. This should not be undertaken by people having chemotherapy or radiotherapy. Be aware that this way of helping to cleanse and revitalise your body can be a very emotional time. Your body will be kick-started into clearing out toxins and with not having to deal with digesting a lot of food, the energy usually used for that purpose will be spent sending toxins to the nearest exit, including the skin. Physically one can experience headaches, diarrhoea or constipation, lethargy and some confusion. These symptoms usually pass in two to three days. A mono-type diet is recommended only if you feel like doing it, it is not an essential requirement and appeals to some people only.

ACUTE OR HEALING DIET

This approach to food is to allow your digestive system a little rest, a change from having to try and digest the many solids and flavours that have become our way of eating. The lesser number of foods we eat at any one time, the more nutrition we can gain. Reading the properties of the lemon will explain why it's recommended to start the day. The only thing to remember about your juices is to not have them too close to meal times. They are a highly concentrated food; if you wish, you can replace a meal with a juice if that's all you feel like.

Salads with your main meal are also left to how you feel. If you wish to have salad, eat it on its own before you have your cooked food. If you wish, it's okay to replace a cooked meal with salad anytime. If you prefer cooked food and some people do feel better eating cooked food, remember you are obtaining some of your live enzymes from your fresh squeezed juices. If you are very thin and feel the cold, eat a good portion of your food in the form of one-pot meals or soups and add well-cooked grains to these dishes. It is not necessary to follow each day's meals as they are written. The menu is just a guideline to allow you to realise there can be variety in a vegan diet.

It is good to meditate early in the morning between your lemon or dandelion coffee and before breakfast. Also exercise in the afternoon and rest or meditate after lunch. A smoothie can fill the gap that can be felt when leaving high protein foods out of your meals. There is a theory that cancer cells feed on extra protein not used up in the system's normal processes.

Use flax seed oil in your dressings but also try to add an extra tablespoon on your food. You may lose weight when first starting to eat this way but usually your weight stabilises soon after. Remember your body is doing its best to rid itself of unwanted toxic material that is in many forms. There is no limit on the quantity of food you eat, only on the mixtures we are in the habit of putting together.

It is recommended that you follow the dietary suggestions for three to four months, definitely for two months.

Then a few more foods can be introduced. High protein foods such as meat, dairy and sugars, saturated fats and white household salt are all hard on our systems. Not the original foods in its natural form, just what commercial enterprises have done to them. Whole untampered food is what the body needs to remain healthy. It has taken years to bring us to an unhealthy state and it can take a little while to revert just using food, but if you incorporate all the other aspects of healthy living, you can rapidly regain health and happiness.

Practice your meditation, sort out your priorities in life, balance your emotional situations and change your environment if necessary. Don't carry anything in your heart except love and try not to judge others. They are on their own path. We do not know what they need to learn.

It is very difficult to estimate the amount of calories and carbohydrates owing to quantity of food eaten; there is no limit to the amount you feel like eating. RDA of carbohydrates and calories are very nearly covered by the juice nutrients. If concerned about calories and carbohydrates check the Nutrient Charts. The 'juice of choice' late in the afternoon has been assessed as carrot, celery and beetroot as beetroot juice and is very important for liver, lungs and blood. You can also add teaspoons of barley grass powder to any juice.

The menus used at The Gawler Foundation vary slightly from the Healing Diet recommended here. There are many dietary requirements needing to be catered for as well as close to sixty meals three times a day to be prepared. This is done by six persons at a time and as the kitchen is a classification A, as in hospitals etc, it requires slightly different techniques to those usually used at home. The recipes are basically the same, just adapted to a more simple domestic approach. Time and effort are important considerations even when you are well, so please use these to fit into your lifestyle.

SUGGESTIONS FOR 2-WEEK HEALING DIET

This 2-week menu is a suggestion of regime only. As long as you really try to have your vegetable juices regularly and keep up the seven per day, the food can be changed around to suit your needs or taste. Just remember to keep it as simple as possible.

MONDAY

ON RISING ⅓ Lemon juice in ⅔ water

½ HOUR LATER Dandelion coffee or juice

BREAKFAST Bowl of porridge adding 1 tbs flax oil, 1 tsp natural sweetener and soy milk

10 AM Carrot juice

11 AM Green juice

12 NOON Carrot, celery and beetroot juice

LUNCH Two rounds of salad sandwiches using wholegrain, spelt or sourdough bread with a spread of hummus or avocado. Better to have only four ingredients. Add some nori seaweed pieces.

3 PM Carrot juice

4 PM Carrot, celery and parsley juice

5 PM Vegetable juice of choice, maybe add green ginger

DINNER Hot noodle and vegetable stir fry. Add some nori pieces.

LATER (AT LEAST 1 HR) Green tea or another dandelion coffee or piece of fruit if required.

Approximately		Protein per g	Calcium per g	Calories per g	Carbohydrates per g
3	Meals	50	398		
7	Juices	38	1063	641	243

TUESDAY

ON RISING ⅓ Lemon juice in ⅔ water

½ HOUR LATER Dandelion coffee or juice

BREAKFAST Porridge or two to three pieces of cut fruit with soy yoghurt and flax oil. Fruit toast if preferred.

10 AM Carrot juice

11 AM Green juice

12 NOON Carrot, celery and beetroot juice

LUNCH Sorj or mountain bread wrap with avocado and sprouts and hummus spread.

3 PM Carrot juice

4 PM Carrot, celery and parsley juice

5 PM Vegetable juice of choice

DINNER Split pea and lentil burgers with brown rice, green leafy vegetables and mustard sauce.

LATER (AT LEAST 1 HR) Green or herb tea or another dandelion coffee.

Approximately		Protein per g	Calcium per g	Calories per g	Carbohydrates per g
3	Meals	40.5	367		
7	Juices	38	1063	641	243

WEDNESDAY

ON RISING ⅓ Lemon juice in ⅔ water

½ HOUR LATER Dandelion coffee

BREAKFAST Bowl of porridge or muesli adding 1 tbs flax oil and apple juice

10 AM Carrot juice

11 AM Green juice

12 NOON Carrot, celery and beetroot juice

LUNCH Salad of mixed greens plus a serving of red cabbage salad or sea vegetable salad. Bread or roll if needed.

3 PM Carrot juice

4 PM Carrot, celery and parsley juice

5 PM Vegetable juice of choice

DINNER Baked potato in jacket, sauerkraut hot or cold, grilled or oven baked tomatoes with green beans and Brussel sprouts.

LATER (AT LEAST 1 HR) Green or herb tea or another dandelion coffee.

Approximately		Protein per g	Calcium per g	Calories per g	Carbohydrates per g
3	Meals	42.5	520		
7	Juices	38	1063	641	243

THURSDAY

ON RISING ⅓ Lemon juice in ⅔ water

½ HOUR LATER Juice or dandelion coffee

BREAKFAST ½ cantelope or some other melon on its own. Don't eat anything else for one hour after.

10 AM Carrot juice

11 AM Green juice

12 NOON Carrot, celery and beetroot juice

LUNCH Asparagus rolls or any other filling you like in sourdough, sorj or mountain bread.

3 PM Carrot juice

4 PM Carrot, celery and parsley juice

5 PM Vegetable juice of choice

DINNER Green salad, vegetable and chickpea curry. Sprinkle of nori and parsley.

LATER (AT LEAST 1 HR) Green or herb tea or another dandelion coffee.

Approximately		Protein per g	Calcium per g	Calories per g	Carbohydrates per g
3	Meals	43	520		
7	Juices	38	1063	641	243

FRIDAY

ON RISING ⅓ Lemon juice in ⅔ water

½ HOUR LATER Dandelion coffee or juice

BREAKFAST Bowl of porridge or muesli adding 1 tbs flax oil, 1 tsp sweetener and soy or oat milk; also add currants.

10 AM Carrot juice

11 AM Green juice

12 NOON Carrot, celery and beetroot juice

LUNCH Two salad sandwiches with a spread of hummus or avocado, adding alfalfa sprouts and shredded nori.

3 PM Carrot juice

4 PM Carrot, celery and parsley juice

5 PM Vegetable juice of choice

DINNER Lemon baked vegetables with broccoli and brown rice.

LATER (AT LEAST 1 HR) Green or herb tea or another dandelion coffee.

Approximately		Protein per g	Calcium per g	Calories per g	Carbohydrates per g
3	Meals	40	357		
7	Juices	38	1063	641	243

SATURDAY

ON RISING ⅓ Lemon juice in ⅔ water

½ HOUR LATER Dandelion coffee or juice

BREAKFAST Muesli soaked in apple juice adding extra oil.

10 AM Carrot juice

11 AM Green juice

12 NOON Carrot, celery and beetroot juice

LUNCH Pizza using pita bread as a base. Top with vegetables of your own preference. Bake in oven or grill till hot.

3 PM Carrot juice

4 PM Carrot, celery and parsley juice

5 PM Vegetable juice of choice

DINNER Potato and corn mustard sauce bake with steamed carrots and cabbage, sprinkle with nori.

LATER (AT LEAST 1 HR) Green or herb tea or another dandelion coffee.

Approximately		Protein per g	Calcium per g	Calories per g	Carbohydrates per g
3	Meals	30	345		
7	Juices	38	1063	641	243

SUNDAY

ON RISING ⅓ Lemon juice in ⅔ water

½ HOUR LATER Dandelion coffee or juice

BREAKFAST Cooked tomatoes, grilled or stewed, served on toast. Can add a slice of marinated tofu underneath tomatoes.

10 AM Carrot juice

11 AM Green juice

12 NOON Carrot, celery and beetroot juice

LUNCH Salad with greens, coleslaw, avocado and sprouts.

3 PM Carrot juice

4 PM Carrot, celery and parsley juice

5 PM Vegetable juice of choice

DINNER Baked tofu slices with steamed bok choy and baked sweet potato.

LATER (AT LEAST 1 HR) Green or herb tea or another dandelion coffee.

Approximately		Protein per g	Calcium per g	Calories per g	Carbohydrates per g
3	Meals	28	579		
7	Juices	38	1063	641	243

PEACH PIE
PAGE 131

ZUCCHINI MOULD
PAGE 90

MONDAY

ON RISING ⅓ Lemon juice in ⅔ water

½ HOUR LATER Dandelion coffee or juice

BREAKFAST Bowl of porridge or muesli adding 1 tbs flax oil, 1 tsp sweetener and soy or oat milk; also add currants.

10 AM Carrot juice

11 AM Green juice

12 NOON Carrot, celery and beetroot juice

LUNCH Large bowl of bean sprout salad and greens. Roll or grain bread of choice.

3 PM Carrot juice

4 PM Carrot, celery and parsley juice

5 PM Vegetable juice of choice

DINNER Mushroom stir-fry and pasta of choice.

LATER (AT LEAST 1 HR) Green or herb tea or another dandelion coffee. Or smoothie.

Approximately		Protein per g	Calcium per g	Calories per g	Carbohydrates per g
3	Meals	52	614		
7	Juices	38	1063	641	243

TUESDAY

ON RISING ⅓ Lemon juice in ⅔ water

½ HOUR LATER Dandelion coffee or juice

BREAKFAST Two to three pieces of cut fruit with soy yoghurt and flax oil. Add a few almonds.

10 AM Carrot juice

11 AM Green juice (plus 1 tsp barley green powder)

12 NOON Carrot, celery and beetroot juice

LUNCH Bowl of broccoli and almond soup with sorj or homemade bread. Or a salad.

3 PM Carrot juice

4 PM Carrot, celery and parsley juice

5 PM Vegetable juice of choice

DINNER Lentil pie served with gravy and lots of green leafy vegetables ie. spinach, bok choy, silver beet or cabbage.

LATER (AT LEAST 1 HR) Green or herb tea or another dandelion coffee.

Approximately		Protein per g	Calcium per g	Calories per g	Carbohydrates per g
3	Meals	35	452		
7	Juices	38	1063	641	243

WEDNESDAY

ON RISING ⅓ Lemon juice in ⅔ water

½ HOUR LATER Dandelion coffee or juice

BREAKFAST Half to one grapefruit or cooked tomatoes on toast.

10 AM Carrot juice

11 AM Green juice (plus 1 tsp barley green powder)

12 NOON Carrot, celery and beetroot juice

LUNCH Rice paper rolls and dipping sauce.

3 PM Carrot juice

4 PM Carrot, celery and parsley juice

5 PM Vegetable juice of choice

DINNER Sweet and sour tofu and vegetables with rice.

LATER (AT LEAST 1 HR) Green or herb tea or another dandelion coffee.

Approximately		Protein per g	Calcium per g	Calories per g	Carbohydrates per g
3	Meals	28	330		
7	Juices	38	1063	641	243

THURSDAY

ON RISING ⅓ Lemon juice in ⅔ water

½ HOUR LATER Dandelion coffee or juice

BREAKFAST Bowl of porridge adding 1 tbs flax oil, currants and almonds with soy or oat milk.

10 AM Carrot juice

11 AM Green juice (plus 1 tsp barley green powder)

12 NOON Carrot, celery and beetroot juice

LUNCH Salad sandwiches using greens, sprouts, tomato and cucumber.

3 PM Carrot juice

4 PM Carrot, celery and parsley juice

5 PM Vegetable juice of choice

DINNER Mushroom stroganoff with polenta.

LATER (AT LEAST 1 HR) Dandelion coffee or smoothie.

Approximately		Protein per g	Calcium per g	Calories per g	Carbohydrates per g
3	Meals	40	403		
7	Juices	38	1063	641	243

FRIDAY

ON RISING ⅓ Lemon juice in ⅔ water

½ HOUR LATER Dandelion coffee or juice

BREAKFAST Bowl of muesli adding 1 tbs flax oil, with apple juice.

10 AM Carrot juice

11 AM Green juice (plus 1 tsp barley green powder)

12 NOON Carrot, celery and beetroot juice

LUNCH Miso or spicy tomato soup and roll or bread. Or salad, if hot.

3 PM Carrot juice

4 PM Carrot, celery and parsley juice

5 PM Vegetable juice of choice

DINNER Zucchini loaf served with oven baked potato, pumpkin and carrot. Brown gravy.

LATER (AT LEAST 1 HR) Green or herb tea or another dandelion coffee.

Approximately		Protein	Calcium	Calories	Carbohydrates
		per g	per g	per g	per g
3	Meals	23	446		
7	Juices	38	1063	641	243

SATURDAY

ON RISING ⅓ Lemon juice in ⅔ water

½ HOUR LATER Dandelion coffee or juice

BREAKFAST Grilled or steamed tomatoes on toast. Or porridge.

10 AM Carrot juice

11 AM Green juice

12 NOON Carrot, celery and beetroot juice

LUNCH Pita bread or roll filled with salad. Add avocado, sprouts and hummus.

3 PM Carrot juice

4 PM Carrot, celery and parsley juice

5 PM Vegetable juice of choice

DINNER Hijike pie served with green beans and scalloped sweet potato.

LATER (AT LEAST 1 HR) Hot carob drink. Herb tea or dandelion coffee.

Approximately		Protein	Calcium	Calories	Carbohydrates
		per g	per g	per g	per g
3	Meals	30	447		
7	Juices	38	1063	641	243

SUNDAY

ON RISING ⅓ Lemon juice in ⅔ water

½ HOUR LATER Dandelion coffee or juice

BREAKFAST Bowl of muesli adding 1 tbs flax oil, apple juice and soy yoghurt.

10 AM Carrot juice

11 AM Green juice (plus 1 tsp barley green powder)

12 NOON Carrot, celery and beetroot juice

LUNCH Mexican pasta salad and rice cakes.

3 PM Carrot juice

4 PM Carrot, celery and parsley juice

5 PM Vegetable juice of choice

DINNER Sliced tofu with ginger served with Asian greens and brown rice.

LATER (AT LEAST 1 HR) Green or herb tea or another dandelion coffee.

Approximately		Protein per g	Calcium per g	Calories per g	Carbohydrates per g
3	Meals	35	582		
7	Juices	38	1063	641	243

NUTRIENT CHARTS

Nutrient Content Charts (except where noted *—100-gram portions)

FOOD	Protein g	Carbohydrates mg	Calcium mg	Iron mg	Saturated Fat g	Digestion Times hrs	Acid/Alkaline	Vitamins
Agar Agar*50 g	2.5	75	200	2.5	-	1.5	Alk	E
Almonds	20	20	200	4.5	-	2.25	Alk	AB
Apple *1	.5	24	12	.5	-	2.75	Alk	ABC
Apricot *3	1	13	18	5	-	2.75	Alk	BC
Asparagus	1	1.5	21	6	-	2.25	Alk	ABC
Alfalfa	5.5	-	28	2.5	-	2	Alk	AB
Avocado	2	6.5	10	5	-	1.75	Alk	ABC
Banana *1	1	20	12	1	-	3	Alk	ABC
Barley	8	80	26	2	-	4	Acid	B
Beetroot	1.5	6	18	1	-	2.75	Alk	ABC
Bread: *1 slice								
Wholewheat	2.5	11	23	5	.11	3	Acid	ABmin
White-enriched	2	11	24	6	18	4	Acid	Bs
Broccoli	2.5	3.5	70	1	-	3	Alk	ABC
Butter	75	.2	23	-	50	3.25	Acid	ADE
Beef	18	-	10	3	4	3.5	Acid	E
Brussel Sprouts	1	5	14	.5	-	4	Alk	ABC
Cabbage	1.5	7	16	.5	-	3	Alk	ABE
Carob Powder	4	60	200	3	-	3	Alk	-
Carrot	1	10	37	.75	-	2.25	Alk	ABCD
Capsicum	1.5	7	16	.5	-	3	Alk	ABC
Cauliflower	3	5	26	1	-	2.25	Alk	ABC

Nutrient Content Charts (except where noted *—100-gram portions)

FOOD	Protein g	Carbohydrates mg	Calcium mg	Iron mg	Saturated Fat g	Digestion Times hrs	Acid/Alkaline	Vitamins
Celery	1	4.5	47	.5	-	3.25	Alk	ABC
Chickpeas	21	62	300	11	.5	3	Acid	BE
Corn	3	25	2.5	.5	-	3	Alk	ABC
Coconut	.5	33	9	1	20	3.25	Acid	ABC
Cucumber	1	3.5	26	1	-	3.25	Alk	ABC
Chicken	12	-	8	1	2	3.25	Acid	E
Cheese:								
Parmesan	9	80	320	20	3	3	Acid	AB
Cottage	13	3	62	14	3	3	Acid	ABCD
Hard	21	210	560	100	18	3	Acid	AB
Dates	2	72	60	3	-	2.5	Alk	ABC
Eggs *1	5.5	.4	24	1	1.5	2.25	Acid	ABE
Fish:								
White/Deep-sea	22	-	10	.5	.25	3	Acid	ABE
Flour:								
Rice	7.5	107	11	6.5	-	3	Acid	ABE
Rye	8	70	20	10	-	3.25	Acid	AB
Soy	43	36	260	9	18	3	Acid	AB
Wholewheat	11.8	9.7	18	.9	-	3	Acid	BDE
Garlic *1 clove	-	.5	-	.5	-	2	Alk	ABC
Grapes	1.5	18	20	.5	-	1.5	Alk	ABC
Grapefruit *(half)	.8	10	14	1	-	3	Alk	BC
Green Bean	1	6.5	30	2	-	3.25	Alk	ABC
Hazelnut	3.7	8	53	1.0	.5	2.5	Acid	BC

Nutrient Content Charts (except where noted *—100-gram portions)

FOOD	Protein g	Carbohydrates mg	Calcium mg	Iron mg	Saturated Fat g	Digestion Times hrs	Acid/Alkaline	Vitamins
Seaweed:								
Nori *2 sheets	2.2	2	13	.5	-	1.5	Alk	ABC
Hijike *50 g	5.5	42	6	2.7	-	1.25	Alk	ABCE
Kombu *50 g	7.5	54	400	5	-	1.5	Alk	ABCE
Kelp *1 tbs	1.5	5.5	156	.5	-	1.25	Alk	ABCE
Lamb	12	-	7	.5	7-10	2	Acid	AB
Leek	2	11	52	1	-	2.5	Alk	ABCE
Lemon *1 tbs	-	1.2	-	1	-	2	Alk	BC
Lentil	19	18	27	3	-	3	Acid	AB
Lettuce	1	3	74	1.5	-	2.25	Alk	ABCE
Lima Bean	8	25	24	4	-	2.25	Alk	BE
Mango	1.1	35	21	.3	-	1.75	Alk	BC
Melon (water)	.5	6	7	.5	-	2	Alk	ABC
Milk: 1 cup = 250 ml								
Cow	3.75	5	130	5.5	2.5	2	Alk	ABCE
Goat	4	5	160	6	3.5	2	Alk	ABCE
Soy	7.7	5	47	1.5	-	2.5	Alk	BC
Whey 10 g	120	6	60	.075	.075	2	Alk	ABC
Miso *50 g	48	107	128	1	-	2	Alk	AB
Millet	11	80	20	7	-	3	Alk	A
Mung Bean Sprouts 1 cup	3	6	14	.9				
Mushroom	2	3	18	3	-	2.5	Alk	AB
Shitake 100 g	0.5	0.5			1			
Oats	2	10	11	.5	-	2.5	Alk	ABE
Olives (black)	1	30	100	1.5	-	1.75	Alk	AE

Nutrient Content Charts (except where noted *—100-gram portions)

FOOD	Protein g	Carbohydrates mg	Calcium mg	Iron mg	Saturated Fat g	Digestion Times hrs	Acid/Alkaline	Vitamins
Onion	1	7	85	1.5	-	3.25	Alk	AE
Orange	1	16	-	-	-	2	Alk	ABCDE
Olive Oil *1 tbs	.5	.5	-	-	1.5	3.25	Alk	ADE
Parsley	4	10	275	7	-	1.5	Alk	B
Parsnip	2	18	50	.5	-	3	Alk	AB
Pasta (wholewheat)	4	32	8	1	-	3	Acid	BE
Pecans	4.5	7	40	1	4	3	Acid	AB
Peas	6	16	18	1.5	-	3.5	Alk	ABC
Peach	.5	10	9	.5	-	2.25	Acid	ABC
Pear	.75	15	8	.2	-	2.25	Acid	B
Potato	2	16	7	.5	-	2	Alk	ABC
Prune	1.5	50	42	3.5	-	3	Acid	AB
Pineapple (1 cup)	.6	19	34	.7	-	2.5	Alk	AB
Pomegranate (1 cup)	1.5	26	58	.5	-	3.25	Acid	BC
Pumpkin	1	10	26	.5	-	3.25	Alk	ABC
Radish	1	3	28	.5	-	3.25	Alk	BC
Rice	2	20	10	.5	-	2	Acid	ABE
Rice (wild)	3.2		2.5	0.5				
Salmon	22	-	260	1.5	1	3.75	Acid	ABC
Sardine	24	-	50	.5	1	3	Acid	AB
Silver beet	2	4	90	2	-	3	Alk	ABCD

Nutrient Content Charts (except where noted *—100-gram portions)

FOOD	Protein g	Carbohydrates mg	Calcium mg	Iron mg	Saturated Fat g	Digestion Times hrs	Acid/Alkaline	Vitamins
Soy Beans	28.6	17	175	8.8	2.2		Alk	
Spinach	2.5	3	80	2	-	2	Alk	ABCD
Spring Onion	0.3	2	4	0.1				
Sweet Potato	1	18	23	.5	-	3.25	Alk	ABC
Sugar	-	1 *(simple)* -		-	-	1.5	Acid	B
Tofu	8	3	250	4	-	3	Alk	B
Tomato	1	7	20	.5	-	2	Acid(raw) Alk(cooked)	ABC
Tomato Paste *(sundried)*	5	25	46	3.9	.2			
Tuna	28	-	16	1.5	-	3	Acid	AB
Yoghurt	4	5.5	135	.5	2.5	2	Alk	AB
Walnut	7	7	45	1.5	2.5	3	Acid	B
Zucchini	.75	2.5	-	.5	-	2.75	Alk	A

Miscellaneous Flavourings

FOOD	Protein g	Carbohydrates mg	Calcium mg	Iron mg	Saturated Fat g	Digestion Times hrs	Acid/Alkaline	Vitamins
Honey 1 tsp	0.1		1	0.1			Acid	
Soy Mayonnaise 2 tbs	.07	.3			1.7			
Cream Dairy 1/2 cup		2.5		75	0.35			Acid
Torula (yeast) 100 g	38.6		424	19.3				
Braggs Bouillon	9.5				.07			

Nutrient Content Charts (except where noted *—100-gram portions)

FOOD	Protein g	Carbohydrates mg	Calcium mg	Iron mg	Saturated Fat g	Digestion Times hrs	Acid/Alkaline	Vitamins
Tamari 1 tbs	1.2		2.4	0.3	1.0			
Ginger fresh 1 tsp	0.1		0.1					
Tahini 1 tsp	2.6		64	1.3				
Basil dried 1 tsp	0.2		30	0.6				
Coriander dried 1 tsp	0.2		13	0.3				
Oregano dried 1 tsp	0.2		24	.7				
Rosemary dried 1tsp	0.1		15	0.4				
Curry Powder	0.3		10	0.6				
Parsley	0.1		4	0.3				

Note: ¼ tsp dried herbs = 1 tsp fresh herbs
2 tsp dried yeast = 25 g compressed fresh yeast

No reliable reference is available where no figure appears in this chart.
These tables were cross-referenced from
• *Nutritional Almanac*, USA
• *Laugh with Health*, Aust
• *Bernard Jensen*, Healing Foods, USA
as they all differed in the nutrient content of each food.

MAINTENANCE DIET

The eating pattern suggested in this book is on two levels or three, if you wish to do a mono diet for a few days. The mono diet can help you on a physical level but also make it clear to you the part food plays in our lives. Something that most often doesn't get a lot of attention, but can be a very powerful part of our lives. With new knowledge of ourselves and our body, we can move to the healing food pattern offered. These recipes give you a variety of foods to choose from to suit your family and lifestyle. It can be challenging but also very empowering. You are taking control of a part of your life. Don't feel restricted to the suggested menus as everyone has different likes and dislikes. There are many foods available that are not chemically damaged. Also try to avoid the microwave. Depending on the climate you live in, your choice of food will differ. The main criteria are fresh well-grown vegetables, grains, fruits, legumes and nuts. Importantly believe that what you are doing is the best you can do and will lead you on the path to wellness. I personally think the best

healing tool we have is on top of our neck, our head creates our world.

You can now move to a more varied intake of food, still remembering the basic principles of good eating, not too much variety in each meal, low consumption of high fat, protein, sugar and salt and some dairy if required. If you are really hungry for flesh you can add some deep-sea fish, tinned tuna, sardines or salmon. Always drain or rinse off the liquid used in the cans. It is still prudent to leave all shellfish out of the diet as they don't call them the scavengers of the sea for nothing. Some people really crave red meat, so if this is you, have a very small serve of good quality lean meat. For example fillet steak, when it is absolutely necessary for your sanity. Organic or bio-dynamic chickens are sometimes necessary but chickens are not the best choice for nutrient value.

It is important to relax and enjoy each meal even if it is not the ideal for you; we are not always going to be able to control our diet. Accept that what you eat most of the time, is the important fact. You don't want to close down the social aspects of your life because others think you are too hard to please. Given the opportunity, hosts will wish to help where they can so let them know in advance of your needs. Take along your juices and a smile and be happy for the company.

What is a maintenance diet anyway? It simply means to keep up the practice you have employed using the healing diet but adding a bigger variety of foods. Not going back on what you have gained; your perception of yourself and your lifestyle will have changed and generally people don't wish to return to a way of life that proved to be unhealthy.

Health can be construed in many ways. It is a word used so much and it means a lot to some and is inconsequential to others. Each must decide for themselves how they want to live. The actual food intake you decide on must be comfortable for you. Your body will not function as you would like if you hate every mouthful of what you eat. Find recipes and food that is good for you and work with that. Learn all you can about yourself and work at being the best you can.

An example of a maintenance diet is not supplied as all you really need to do is use the other recipes in this book and add a few of your own, keeping within the guidelines. There are a few recipes for fish included but I am sure you will find plenty to add. Keep up your juices as best you can, eat plenty of green foods, chew your grains well and try to still eat simple combinations of foods at any given meal.

Soy products are useful but if for any reason you are not comfortable using them, you don't really need to. Just make up extra protein with other foods. See the chart for information.

RECIPES

Vegetable recipes

CORN PIE (Serves 4)

2½ cups mashed potato, for the pie shell
2 cups corn kernels
1 diced tomato
1 diced capsicum
2 sticks chopped celery
6 small sliced mushrooms
1 tsp curry powder
1 tsp Herbamare
1 cup breadcrumbs (not wheat)

Line a pie plate with the mashed potato, bake at 180°C for 15 minutes, meanwhile prepare the other vegetables, mix all these ingredients (except ½ cup breadcrumbs) together and spoon into potato pie shell, sprinkle breadcrumbs over the top, bake at 180°C degrees for 20 minutes.

Per Serve
Protein 7.5 g
Calcium 45 mg
Iron 2 mg
Wheat, Dairy and Egg-free

HOT NOODLES AND VEGETABLES (Serves 4)

1 cup carrots finely sliced
1 cup snow peas finely sliced
1 cup spring onion finely sliced
1 cup red capsicum finely sliced
1 cup cabbage finely sliced
2 tbs grated green ginger
1 tsp crushed garlic
2 tbs tamari or soy sauce
1 cup almonds
1 × 250 g packet rice pasta spirals
Parsley

Boil pasta according to directions on packet. Steam or parboil carrots, cabbage, capsicum, snow peas and spring onions. Add ginger, garlic, soy sauce and almonds. Stir through pasta, top with parsley.

Per Serve
Protein 14 g
Calcium 140 mg
Iron 3 mg
Wheat, Dairy and Egg-free

LEMON BAKED VEGETABLES
(Serves 4)

2 large brown onions
1 medium sweet potato cut into chunky pieces
4 small potatoes cut in quarters
2 parsnips cut into chunky pieces
2 medium lemons
8 small carrots cut into chunky pieces
4 unpeeled cloves garlic
6 sprigs fresh rosemary

Cut onions and lemons into eight wedges. Place onion, lemon, carrot, potatoes, sweet potatoes, parsnips, garlic and rosemary in a baking dish. Bake covered for about ¾ hour or until tender. Remove cover. Increase oven temperature to hot. Turn over the vegetables. Bake about 20 minutes or until brown. Serve with green leafy vegetables and a cooked grain.

Per Serve
Protein 6 g
Calcium 106 mg
Iron 2.5 mg

MIXED RICE BAKE (Serves 4)

1 tbs brown mustard seeds
1 tsp ground coriander
1 tsp tumeric
1 cup long grain brown rice
1 cup wild rice
1 cup hazelnuts
6 cups water or vegetable stock

1½ cups sliced mushrooms
1 diced onion
1 block tofu, cubed small
2 tbs tamari
½ tsp each of basil and thyme

Dry roast hazelnuts in a pan on top of the stove or in a hot oven. Place rice in water in a casserole dish. Layer rest of ingredients and roasted hazelnuts over rice, do not stir. Cover and bake till all water has been absorbed about 1½ hours in 180°C oven.

Per Serve
Protein 8 g
Calcium 190 mg
Iron 3 mg
Wheat, Dairy and Egg-free

MUSHROOM STIR-FRY
(Serves 2)

6 shiitake mushrooms
2 tbs water + 1 tbs tamari
½ cup soaked then chopped arame or hijiki
1 cup diagonally sliced carrots
1 cup bamboo shoots
1 cup snow peas
¼ tsp kelp powder
2 tbs rice vinegar or cider vinegar

Soak shiitake mushrooms and aname in warm water for 15 minutes, slice mushrooms, chop arame or hijiki. Sauté arame and carrots in water and tamari for 5 minutes, add other vegetables, cook till tender but not mushy, add kelp and vinegar. Serve with rice.

Per Serve
Protein 3.5 g
Calcium 92 mg
Iron 2 mg
Wheat, Dairy and Egg-free

MUSHROOM STROGANOFF
(Serves 4)

1 large onion diced
½ green pepper sliced
1 cup sliced celery
4 cups chopped mushrooms
1 tbs rice flour
1 cup water
1 tbs yeast flakes
¼ cup yoghurt
2 tsp tamari
½ tsp thyme
2 tbs chopped parsley
1 dsp corn flour mixed with cold water to a thin paste
1 cup diced tofu (optional)

Sauté onions in a little water, add celery, pepper and mushrooms. Cook 5 minutes. Stir in rice flour, add water, yeast flakes and thyme. Bring to the boil and simmer for 3 minutes. Add parsley and thickening and boil for 1 minute. Remove from heat and stir in yoghurt and tamari. Serve over rice or pasta.

Per Serve
Protein 5.5 g
Calcium 71 mg
Iron 2.5 mg

Wheat, Dairy and Egg-free
(if using soy yoghurt)

POTATO CAKES

Potatoes   2 tbs water
Egg white
Crumbs—can use wholemeal bread, spelt bread, corn crisp bread (crushed), rice flour.

Scrub required amount of potatoes. Cut into 1 cm thick slices. Steam for 5 minutes. Beat 1 egg white with 2 tbs water. Dip slices in mixture and then coat in the crumbs of your choice. Place on a greased oven tray and bake in a hot oven for 10–15 minutes until nicely browned, turning once.

Per Serve
Protein 3.5 g
Calcium 37 mg
Iron 1 mg

POTATO PIE (Serves 4)

1 kg potatoes
2 onions
500 g eggplant diced
1 tbs chopped parsley
3 tbs soy or oat milk
3 medium tomatoes diced
1 green capsicum diced
½ tsp basil
½ tsp crushed garlic
¼ cup water

Boil and then mash potatoes with the soy milk. Set aside. Sauté onion and garlic in the water, add remaining ingredients, cook 2–3 minutes, place in casserole dish, top with mashed potatoes. Bake at 180°C for 15–20 minutes.

Per Serve
Protein 3.5 g
Calcium 82 mg
Iron 4.5 mg
Wheat, Dairy and Egg-free

PUMPKIN, CAULIFLOWER AND CHICKPEA HOT POT (Serves 4–6)

1 cup chickpeas soaked overnight
1 kg butternut pumpkin cubed
1 medium parsnip cubed
1 chopped red capsicum
1 onion sliced
1 zucchini
2 cups cauliflower
1 tsp coriander
1 tsp cumin
1 tsp tumeric
1 cup chopped tomatoes
1 tbs tomato puree
200 ml water
1 tbs Braggs boullion
1 tbs fresh chopped coriander

Cook chickpeas. Sprinkle spices over vegetables—butternut, parsnip, capsicum and zucchini, onion and cauliflower, cover and bake 45 minutes. Add chickpeas, tomatoes, tomato puree, water and Braggs, heat through in the oven. Stir in fresh coriander and check seasonings.

PUMPKIN AND POTATO CASSEROLE (Serves 4)

Casserole:
4 cups each of thinly sliced potato and pumpkin

In a lightly greased casserole dish, place a little sauce, then alternate layers of potato and pumpkin (sprinkling the pumpkin lightly with Herbamare), finishing with pumpkin. Pour remainder of sauce over vegetables. Cover casserole dish with a lid and bake in a moderate oven for about 45 minutes or until vegetables are tender.

White Sauce:
2 cups soy milk
1 cup water
1 large onion diced
1 bay leaf
2 tsp hot English mustard
½ tsp Herbamare or to taste
2 dsp cornflour (mixed to a thin cream with cold water)

Boil the onion in water. When transparent, add soy milk, Herbamare, bay leaf and mustard. Bring back to boil, thicken with cornflour mix and let boil again for 1 minute.

Per Serve
Protein 10 g
Calcium 98 mg
Iron 3 mg
Wheat, Dairy and Egg-free

QUINOA LOAF (Serves 4)

3 cups cooked quinoa
1 cup spelt or wholewheat flour
½ cup warm water
1 tbs barley miso
1 tbs lecithin granules
1 tsp each basil and thyme
1 onion chopped
2 cups carrots diced
2 cups broccoli diced
2 cups parsley chopped
1 cup almonds chopped

Dissolve miso and lecithin in the warm water and mix into quinoa and flour and herbs. Place onion, carrots and broccoli in a steamer and cook for 10 minutes. Mix quinoa and vegetables together gently and place in lightly oiled loaf pan. Sprinkle almonds on top and bake for 40 minutes at 200°C. Turn out and garnish with parsley.

RÖSTI (Serves 4–6)

1½ kg potatoes
4 tbs olive oil
2 tbs spring onion chopped
½ tsp sea salt

Scrub, then boil the potatoes in their skins. Allow them to cool thoroughly and grate coarsely. Heat oil in a large pan and add potatoes which have been mixed with salt and onion. Cook on a low to medium heat until underneath is browned (lift one side to check), slide onto a greased plate and return to pan upside down to cook and brown on the other side. Cut into wedges to serve.

Per Serve
Protein 14 g
Calcium 26 mg
Iron 2 mg

SAUERKRAUT (1) (Serves 2–4)

2 cups red cabbage chopped
1 cup green cabbage chopped
1 clove garlic chopped
2 tsp honey
1 tbs red onion chopped
1 tsp dill seeds or tips
1 tbs apple cider vinegar
1 cup water

Combine cabbages, garlic, onion, dill seeds and water. Cook gently for a few minutes. Add apple cider vinegar and honey, cook until cabbage is soft. Can be served hot or cold.

Per Serve
Protein 4.5 g
Calcium 51 mg
Iron 7 mg
Wheat Egg and Dairy-free

SAUERKRAUT (2)

1 firm green cabbage, chopped roughly
½ large red onion, chopped
2 garlic cloves, pressed

1½ tbs dill weed

Can add 2 tsp of celery or caraway seed for a different flavour

Wash and clean the vegetables, remove a few outer leaves to be used as a cover for the sauerkraut. Grate the vegetables in a food processor. Make as much juice as possible by squeezing the vegetables; this is the medium which activates the fermentation. Put all the vegetables and spices in a large bowl, mix and then place them in a crock-type container. Pack down well with your hands to get all the air out. Cover vegetables with the cabbage leaves, pressing down hard. Place a plate that fits inside the container, on top of the cabbage leaves. Weigh down the plate with a glass jar of water or any item that will keep the plate pressed down. Cover with a towel and leave in a warm spot in your kitchen. Test for a zesty flavour after 4 days. Should take a maximum of 7 days to be ready. Remove the plate when the sauerkraut is ready and also any discoloured cabbage on the top. Remove to glass jars, cap the jars and keep in the fridge; good for several months. Live sauerkraut is rich in lactic acid. Lactic acid feeds the good bacteria in the bowel, also necessary for vitality and growth of new cells. It assists in detoxifying and cleansing your system.

SCALLOPED SWEET POTATOES (Serves 2–3)

1 large sweet potato unpeeled and sliced
2 large red onions thinly sliced
1 cup soy milk
1 clove garlic

Lay slices of sweet potato in greased baking dish. Add sliced onion over potatoes. Mix crushed garlic into soy milk. Pour over potatoes. Cook in moderate oven 180°C covered for first 30 minutes, uncovered for last 15 minutes—totalling ¾ hour.

Per Serve
Protein 7 g
Calcium 105 mg
Iron 3 mg

SIMPLE KOMBU VEGETABLE BAKE (Serves 2–3)

48–50 cm Kombu—approx 3 sticks, soaked for at least 12 hours, cut in 2 cm squares
3 cups carrots sliced
2 cups turnips diced
2 cups cabbage shredded

Sauce:
½ cup water
1 tbs minced or grated ginger
3 tbs tamari

Mix all sauce ingredients together. Layer vegetables in a baking pan, starting with Kombu, dash each layer with some sauce. Cover and bake for 1 hour at 180°C. Serve with a grain or pasta.

Per Serve
Protein 4 g
Calcium 160 mg
Iron 2 mg
Wheat, Dairy and Egg-free

SPICY POTATOES (Serves 3–4)

1 kg potatoes cut in wedges
1 cup undrained canned tomatoes
2 cups chopped or sliced onion
1 dsp crushed garlic
2 tsp mild or sweet chilli powder
1 cup chopped parsley
1 tsp Herbamare

Lightly cook potatoes by steaming or boiling, do not cook through. Sauté the onion, add garlic and seasoning, then tomatoes. Add potatoes and cook gently for another 12–15 minutes. Serve with a frittata type dish, sprinkled with chopped parsley.

Per Serve
Protein 5 g
Calcium 33 mg
Iron .5 mg
Wheat, Dairy and Egg-free

STUFFED POTATOES (1) (Serves 4)

4 large potatoes
150 g tofu
2 spring onions chopped
1 cup corn kernels
1 cup sweet potato diced
1 tsp Herbamare

Scrub and prick potatoes. Cook in oven, covered for first 30 minutes, uncovered for another 30 minutes, or steam whole. Cook and mash sweet potato. Mash tofu. Mix tofu, spring onion, sweet potato, corn and Herbamare. Cut top off potatoes, scoop out centre and mash in with tofu etc. Pile back into potato shells. Return to oven 200°C to reheat for 15–20 minutes. Sprinkle with favourite herbs.

Per Serve
Protein 8 g
Calcium 110 mg
Iron 3 mg
Wheat, Dairy and Egg-free

STUFFED POTATOES (2) (Serves 4)

4 good-sized potatoes
1 cup finely chopped onions
1 cup finely chopped mushrooms
1 cup cooked mashed sweet potato
½ tsp savoury or herb of choice
2 tbs barley or rice miso
2 tbs chopped parsley
pinch of sweet paprika

Scrub and bake the potatoes for 1 hour at 180°C or until cooked. Sauté onion and mushrooms with herbs, set aside. When potatoes are done, cut in half and scoop out the centre leaving 1 cm of potato in shell. Mash scooped out potato and other vegetables together with seasoning. Put back into shell and top with paprika. Return to oven to reheat and brown on top.

Per Serve
Protein 7 g
Calcium 52 mg
Iron 2 mg
Wheat, Dairy and Egg-free

SUMMER VEGETABLE MOULDS
(Serves 4)

2 very ripe tomatoes chopped
2 cups tomato juice
3 tbs agar agar
1 capsicum chopped
2 cups cooked peas
1 cup corn kernels
1 tbs chopped parsley

Heat juice and add agar agar, stir constantly, bring to boil and simmer for 1 minute. Cool, stir in the rest of the ingredients. Pour into individual moulds and allow to set. Turn out onto a bed of shredded lettuce and decorate with sliced tomato or avocado.

Sauce:
2 cups plain yoghurt
½ cups yeast flakes
1 tsp mustard
½ tsp Herbamare

Blend all together. Serve over moulds.

Per Serve
Protein 12 g
Calcium 213 mg
Iron 4.5 mg
Wheat and Egg-free
Dairy-free (if using soy yoghurt)

SWEET CORN PATTIES
(Serves 4)

1 cup buckwheat flour
1 cup rice flour
2 tsp curry powder
1 large onion
1½ cups corn kernels
2 tbs chopped parsley
1 egg
1 tsp Herbamare
1½ cups milk (soy or oat)

Mix flours together. Beat egg and milk. Mix all together. Cook in spoonfuls on lightly greased grill or frying pan turning once.

Per Serve
Protein 15 g
Calcium 45 mg
Iron 4 mg
Wheat-free Dairy-free

TOMATO AND ONION SIDE DISH (Serves 3–4)

6–8 tomatoes
4 onions
2 cups seasoned bread crumbs

Slice tomatoes. Peel and thickly slice onions. Place ¾ tomatoes in a greased casserole dish, place onions on top followed by the rest of the tomatoes. Cover all with seasoned breadcrumbs, cover casserole and bake for about ¾ hour in 180°C oven.

VEGETABLE AND CHICKPEA CURRY (Serves 4)

2 tbs olive oil
2 tbs water
1 cup brown onion thinly sliced
1 tbs grated fresh ginger
1 dsp garlic crushed
½ tsp dried tumeric
2 tsp ground coriander
2 tsp garam masala
2 potatoes cut into 2 cm cubes
2 carrots cut into 2 cm slices
2 zucchini, cut into 2 cm slices
2 cups tomatoes chopped
1½ cups reduced salt vegetable stock or 3 stock cubes dissolved in 1½ cups water
400 g can chickpeas, rinsed and drained
2 cups baby spinach leaves, washed
1 cup fresh or frozen peas
1½ cups basmati rice
Papadums to serve

Heat oil in a large pot, add the onion and ginger and cook over a medium heat for 5 minutes or until soft. Add the water, garlic and spices and cook for 2 minutes or until fragrant. Add the potatoes and carrots and cook until the vegetables are coated in the spices. Stir in the zucchini, tomatoes and stock and simmer. Reduce heat and cook uncovered for 15 minutes or until the vegetables are tender and the curry has thickened slightly. Add the chickpeas and stir. Add spinach and peas; cook just until the spinach wilts and the peas are soft. Meanwhile cook the rice in boiling water over a high heat until tunnels appear in the rice. Reduce heat to very low, cover and allow to steam for 10 minutes or until the rice is tender and all the liquid is absorbed. Serve the curry on top of the rice and accompany with the papadums.

Per Serve
Protein 30 g
Calcium 257 mg
Iron 10 mg
Wheat, Dairy and Egg-free

VEGETABLE CHOICE PIE

Carrots
Chickpeas or other legumes
Diced pumpkin
Potatoes
Peas or corn
Soy sauce
Herbs of choice

Peel off thin strips of carrot with a vegetable peeler and line a greased pie plate or individual heatproof bowls with the carrot strips. Fill plate or bowls with cooked (or tinned) chickpeas or beans, diced pumpkin, potatoes and peas or corn. Sprinkle with soy sauce or herbs of your choice, grate potato over the top of vegetables and cook in a moderate oven 180°C for 45 minutes. Pies can be turned upside down on a serving plate. Serve with broccoli and green beans, brown rice or pasta.

Wheat, Dairy and Egg-free

VEGETABLE NUT LOAF
(Serves 4)

1 cup wholemeal or spelt fresh bread-crumbs
3 cups mixed vegetables diced finely
1 cup ground or chopped almonds
½ tsp sage
1 tsp Herbamare
2 eggs
1 cup milk of choice (soy or oat)

Mix eggs and milk well. Add to the rest of the ingredients. Pack tightly into a greased loaf pan. Bake in moderate oven 180°C for 45 minutes.

Per Serve
Protein 10.5 g
Calcium 258 mg
Iron 6 mg

VEGETABLE SAUSAGES

2 cups cooked rice
2 cups cooked chickpeas pureed in blender or food processor
1 cup onions chopped

2 cups sweet potato
1 cup parsnip
½–¾ cup rice flour, enough to make a firm mix

Seasoning A:
2 tsp curry powder
1 tsp coriander
1 tsp cumin
1 tbs tamari or Braggs
Herbamare to taste
1–2 tsp crushed garlic

Seasoning B:
cook 2 extra cups of onions and puree
½ cup of tomato puree or
1 cup of tomatoes diced
2 tsp basil
2 tsp mixed herbs

Lightly steam sweet potato, onions and parsnip. Remove from steamer then mash roughly and add to pureed chick-peas. Once mixed all together add the rice flour and seasonings (A or B). Pipe mixture through a pastry bag without star nozzle in place. Cut piped sausages into 9–10 cm lengths. Roll in polenta or flour. Place on greased tray and heat in oven 180°C for 15 minutes turning as they brown.

Per Serve
Protein 82.5 g
Calcium 556 mg
Iron 23.5 mg

ZUCCHINI LOAF (Serves 4)

2 cups cooked brown rice
2 cups broccoli flowerets
500 g zucchini—sliced
raw zucchini to line tray
½ bunch chopped spring onions
½ cup ground almonds
2 tsp chopped garlic
2 tsp curry powder
½ cup soy flour
3 tbs tamari

Steam zucchini and broccoli. Squeeze out excess moisture in zucchini. Mix all other ingredients together then mix in the zucchini and broccoli. Line a greased loaf pan with thin long strips of raw zucchini bottom and sides. Spoon in the rice mixture, pat down well and bake at 190°C for 35 minutes. Allow to cool a little before turning out. This mixture looks good when baked in individual dariole molds.

Per Serve
Protein 6 g
Calcium 75 mg
Iron 3.5 mg
Wheat, Dairy and Egg-free

Grains and pulse recipes

BAKED PUMPKIN AND TEMPEH RISOTTO (Serves 4)

2 cups Arborio rice or brown rice
3–4 vegetable cubes dissolved in 4 cups water
1 tbs olive oil
3 cups jap or butternut pumpkin peeled and finely diced
½ block tempeh
½ cup nutritional yeast flakes
1 tbs chopped parsley
2 cups spinach roughly chopped

Preheat oven to 200°C. Place rice, stock, oil and pumpkin in an ovenproof dish and cover tightly with lid. Bake for 30 minutes or until the rice is soft—the risotto may be quite liquid. Chop tempeh and grill or sauté for approximately 10 minutes. Then, add the yeast flakes, spinach, parsley and stir for 2 minutes and serve.

Per Serve
Protein 7 g
Calcium 118 mg
Iron 1 mg
Saturated Fat 5 g
Wheat, Dairy and Egg-free

BEANS AND RICE (Serves 4)

3 cups cooked rice
1 cup tomatoes diced
2 onions diced

2 zucchini diced
1 cup corn kernels
1 stalk celery chopped
3 tbs tomato puree
2 cups cooked beans of choice (cannelloni, adzuki, borlotti or haricot)

Mix all ingredients except rice together. Cook on stove top in ½ cup water for 15 minutes, or bake covered, in the oven for 45 minutes. Serve with the rice.

Per Serve
Protein 6.5 g
Calcium 55 mg
Iron 2.7 mg
Wheat, Dairy and Egg-free

CHICKPEA AND VEGETABLE ROLLS OR PARTY PIES
(Makes 15–18)

2 sheets shortcrust pastry, rolled to 30 cm long
Cut into 4 strips or into rounds to fit into patty or muffin tins—line greased tins with round pastry bases
3 cups cooked chickpeas roughly mashed
1 medium onion chopped finely
1 cup each of chopped zucchini, celery and tomato
1 tsp chopped garlic
1 tsp Herbamare
2 tsp basil or mixed herbs of choice
½ cup chopped sun dried tomatoes
1 tbs soy mayonnaise
1 cup cooked brown rice

Optional extra:
1 small can of tuna or salmon

Lightly steam all vegetables, add seasonings and chickpeas and mix well. Fill patty tins and cover each pie with another round of pastry. Brush tops with a little egg yolk or milk. Cook for approximately 20 minutes at 200°C. For vegetable rolls, lay filling along the centre of each strip of pastry. Damp top edge of pastry with water and roll up. Cut each roll into six and cook as for party pies. Serve with your favourite dipping sauce.

Per Serve
Protein 11.5 g
Calcium 83 mg
Iron 4 mg
Saturated Fat 2 g
Dairy and Egg-free

CHICKPEA LOAF (Serves 4)

1 cup chickpeas—cooked = 2 cups (can use canned which will equal 2 cups)
1 cup vegetable juice (retained from cooked vegetables not from canned chickpeas)
¾ cup almonds chopped
1 cup each celery, hulled millet and onion
2 tbs parsley
1 egg (optional)
Herbamare

Soak chickpeas overnight if using dried peas. Strain off the soak water, add fresh water and cook until soft. Cook celery with millet and onion in 3 cups water, strain, reserving 1 cup of liquid. Mash chickpeas with this cup of liquid and season with Herbamare. Mix peas, almonds and vegetables together, add egg if required to bind, pack into a greased loaf pan and bake at 160°C for 45 minutes.

Per Serve
Protein 25 g
Calcium 146 mg
Iron 8 mg
Wheat and Dairy-free

GREEK-STYLE PILAF (Serves 4)

1 cup cooked bulghar wheat
1 cup cooked rice
½ finely chopped onion
1 tsp crushed garlic
1 cup finely chopped celery
¼ cup sunflower seeds
1 tsp olive oil (optional)
2 tsp chopped fresh mint
¼ cup chopped parsley
Juice of 1 lemon

Sauté onion, garlic, celery and sunflower seeds in a little water for 5 minutes, add all other ingredients. Can be rolled in vine leaves and poached in a vegetable broth for 15 minutes or bake covered for 25 minutes in 180°C oven.

Per Serve
Protein 1 g
Calcium 45 mg
Iron 1.25 mg
Dairy and Egg-free

GREEN RICE BALLS
(Serve with beans and sage)
(Makes 24 balls)

3 cups cooked brown rice
3 cups cooked finely chopped greens (spinach or silver beet)
6 spring onions chopped
2 tsp dried dill
1½ tbs lemon juice
1 tsp Herbamare
1–2 cups breadcrumbs or seasoned chopped oats.

Cook rice and drain, steam greens then chop. Sauté onion in a little water till brownish. Mix all ingredients together except crumbs, shape teaspoonful into balls, roll in crumbs, and place on greased tray. Bake at 200°C for approximately 20 minutes.

Per Serve
Protein 14.5 g
Calcium 236 mg
Iron 14 mg
Wheat, Dairy and Egg-free

HIJIKI PIE (Serves 4)

Base:
¾ cup rice flour
¾ cup rolled millet flakes
1 tbs savoury nutritional yeast flakes or 1 vegetable cube
5–6 tbs water (if using cube, dissolve in water)

Filling:

½ cup chopped hijiki

2 onions

2 cloves garlic

1 tsp fresh ginger

2 cups pumpkin diced

2 cups mixed vegetables of choice

2 tbs tamari or soy sauce

2 tsp chopped basil

Topping:

½ cup ground almonds

½ cup rice flour

½ cup millet flour

1 dsp each chives or chopped spring onions, basil, herbs

Tamari

⅓ cup water

For base, mix flour and flakes with seasoning and water. Pat into a lightly greased 23 cm pie plate to make the crust. Lightly steam the vegetables. Add other filling ingredients to vegetables and pile into shell. Mix topping ingredients to a crumble and sprinkle over the pie filling. Bake at 180°C for approximately 30 minutes.

Per Serve

Protein 12 g

Calcium 133 mg

Iron 3 mg

Wheat, Dairy and Egg-free

ITALIAN BEANS (Serves 4)

3 cups cooked small beans of choice

2½ cups chopped tomatoes (if using canned drain them)

1–2 tbs chopped fresh sage

1 tbs garlic

1½ tsp lemon juice

½ tsp Herbamare

Sauté garlic and sage in a little water. Add other ingredients, heat through gently.

Per Serve

Protein 13 g

Calcium 90 mg

Iron 6.5 mg

Wheat, Dairy and Egg-free

LENTIL PIE (Serves 4)

Base:

1½ cups organic brown rice

½ cup savoury nutritional yeast flakes

½ cup rice flour

Filling:

400 g sweet potato (gold) diced

2 leeks chopped

500 ml stock or water

50 g button mushrooms

1½ cups brown, green or red lentils

1 tsp crushed garlic

½ cup chopped, soaked arame seaweed

2 tbs chopped, fresh coriander or 1 tsp dried

1 tsp cumin powder

1 tsp Herbamare or 1 dsp soy sauce

Topping:

1 cup oatmeal

2 tsp mixed herbs

2 tsp yeast flakes

Mix together topping. Preheat oven to 200°C. Cook the rice in plenty of water until quite soft. Drain, don't rinse. Add flakes and rice flour. Line a 20 cm greased pie dish, base and sides with the rice mixture. Blind bake for 15 minutes. Sauté the leeks in a little water, add 500 ml (2½ cups) of water or stock. Add lentils and cook 25 minutes. Add mushrooms and sweet potato, cook 5 minutes then add seasonings and arame, stirring occasionally. Pile mix into rice base and sprinkle on topping. Bake in oven 30 minutes until hot and brown on top.

Per Serve

Protein 18 g

Calcium 85 mg

Iron 4.6 mg

Wheat, Dairy and Egg-free

LENTIL ROLLS (Serves 3–4)

3 cups cooked brown lentils

3 cups cooked, lightly mashed, mixed vegetables, eg. (broccoli, carrots, parsnips and potatoes)

1 chopped onion, cooked or ½ cup chopped spring onions

1 tbs tamari

Any other seasoning of choice

4 sheets filo pastry or 4 pieces mountain bread

This mix can be cooked in individual moulds with sauce when serving. Cook in oven approximately 30 minutes. Unmould onto a bed of lettuce and decorate with slices of tomato etc. For pastry rolls mix all ingredients together and roll up on filo pastry as for sausage rolls. The same if using mountain bread. Cut in 5 cm logs. Bake for 15–20 minutes at 180°C.

Tomato Yoghurt Sauce:

1 cup yoghurt

1 tsp crushed garlic

½ tsp mustard (hot English)

¾ cup sundried tomatoes chopped

Use a food wand or processor to mix garlic, mustard and tomatoes. Mix into yoghurt.

Protein 92 g

Calcium 586 mg

Iron 48 mg

Egg and Dairy-free

LIMA BEAN LOAF

2 cups lima beans

½ cup soft breadcrumbs

½ cup chopped parsley

½ tsp chopped garlic

1 tsp Herbamare

½ tsp sage

½ cup tomato juice

2 beaten eggs

1 tbs olive oil (optional)

Soak lima beans overnight in cold water. Drain and cook in fresh water until soft.

Drain and mash beans roughly and mix with all other ingredients. Place in a lightly greased loaf pan in moderate oven 180°C for 35–40 minutes. Serve with green vegetables or a salad.

Per Serve
Protein 18 g
Calcium 67 mg
Iron 3 mg
Dairy-free
Wheat-free (if using rice bread or gluten free bread)

MILLET AND TOFU BURGERS (Serves 4)

3 cups cooked millet or rice
1 cup carrot finely grated
1 onion chopped
1 clove garlic chopped
1 cup crumbled tofu
¼ cup whole grain breadcrumbs
½ cup ground almonds
1 tbs tamari
¾ tsp thyme or marjoram
1 tsp sage

Lightly sauté carrot, garlic and onion in water. Cover and cook on low heat for 5 minutes. In a bowl mix with other ingredients. Shape into burgers. If too crumbly add a little water till they hold together well. Bake on a greased oven tray until browned turning once (approximately 20 minutes).

Per Serve
Protein 26 g
Calcium 118 mg
Iron 14.5 mg

Dairy and Egg-free
Wheat-free (if using rice breadcrumbs)

MUESLI (Serves 2)

2 cups rolled oats or mixture of flaked grains
½ cup sultanas
½ cup currants
½ cup almonds roughly chopped
1 cup biodynamic apple or pear juice

Mix all dry ingredients well. Store in a covered jar until ready for use. Pour juice over muesli and allow to soak for a short while before eating. Top with yoghurt or fruit.

Per Serve
Protein 19 g
Calcium 118 mg
Iron 14 mg
Wheat and Egg-free

PORRIDGE (Serves 2)

½ cup rolled oats
¼ cup rolled barley
¼ cup rolled triticale
1 dsp linseeds

Soak ingredients, except linseeds, overnight in cold water (enough to cover them 5 cm over). In the morning cook over a gentle heat. Stir constantly, adding more water to enable porridge to fall off spoon easily. While the porridge is cooking, crush the linseeds and add to the porridge. Stir well and serve.

SPLIT PEAS AND LENTIL BURGERS (Serves 4)

1 cup brown lentils
1 cup yellow split peas
1 grated onion
3 tsp fresh thyme
1 cup breadcrumbs
2 tsp mustard
2 tsp horseradish cream

Cover lentils and split peas with water and cook until tender. Drain. Sauté the onions. Puree half the lentils and split peas until combined. Remove from blender and place in bowl. Add the remaining peas, lentils, sautéed onion, breadcrumbs, mustard and thyme. Mix well—if too wet add a little rice flour. Make burgers and place on greased trays. Cook for ½ hour in medium oven 180°C. Serve with mustard sauce.

Mustard Sauce:
3 tbs soy mayonnaise
2 tsp horseradish cream
1 tsp prepared mustard (hot English)
Mix together well.

Per Serve
Protein 20 g
Calcium 50 mg
Iron 4.5 mg
Dairy and Egg-free
Wheat-free (if using rice bread)

SWEET AND SOUR CHICKPEAS (Serves 4)

4 cups cooked chickpeas
2 cups onions chopped
1 cup red capsicum chopped
1 tsp chopped garlic
¾ cup water
1 cup sliced celery
½ cup tomato puree
½ cup homemade mirin or bottled sweet and sour sauce
1 tbs arrowroot mixed with 2 tbs of water

Combine all ingredients except arrowroot and ¼ cup water which has been mixed together. Mix the vegetables and peas gently and simmer for 15 minutes in the ¾ cup water, add arrowroot mix and stir gently till boiling, boil for 1 minute. Serve hot over brown rice.

Per Serve
Protein 12 g
Calcium 236 mg
Iron 6.5 mg
Wheat, Dairy and Egg-free

Tofu recipes

CHOW MEIN WITH TOFU OR TEMPEH (Serves 4)

400 g rice noodles, cooked and drained—plunge back into fresh boiling water for 20 seconds prior to serving

Sauce:

4 cups water

2 tsp or 2 cubes vegetable powder

1 onion

5 shiitake mushrooms soaked and sliced

2 cups firm tofu or tempeh cubed

1 cup celery sliced diagonally

1 cup Chinese cabbage shredded

2 cups mung sprouts or bean shoots

small broccoli head roughly chopped

2 tbs kuzu or corn flour dissolved in ⅓ cup water

tamari to taste

Dissolve vegetable powder in the 4 cups water. Add onions and mushrooms. Simmer for 7 minutes. Add tofu or tempeh, simmer for another 5 minutes. Add celery, cabbage, sprouts, broccoli, kuzu and tamari, simmer for about 10 minutes or until thickened. Serve over the heated noodles.

Per Serve
Protein 12 g
Calcium 310 mg
Iron 6 mg
Wheat, Dairy and Egg-free

SLICED TOFU WITH GINGER (Serves 4)

300 g tofu

Tamari

Water

1 teaspoon grated green ginger

1 medium brown onion diced

Cut tofu into slices eg. 10 cm × 7 cm × 1.5 cm thick. Place in a baking dish with finely grated ginger and diced brown onions on top. Add a mixture of 50/50 tamari with water. Pour on to just cover the tofu and bake for 10 minutes in a hot oven or until browning on top. Serve with steamed green leafy vegetables and brown rice.

Per Serve
Protein 4 g
Calcium 70 mg
Iron 1 mg
Wheat, Dairy and Egg-free

TEMPEH STIR-FRY (Serves 4)

1 block unseasoned tempeh

1 cup each of sliced cabbage, broccoli, carrots, zucchini and sweet potato or pumpkin

1 onion chopped

2 cloves garlic crushed

½ cup water

Juice 1 lemon

1 tbs tamari or soy sauce

Cut tempeh into 1 cm blocks

Sauté in ½ cup tamari and ½ cup water adding onion and garlic. Simmer for 10 minutes. Add vegetables (and 2 extra tbs water if needed), and simmer with lid on for 5–10 minutes until cooked but still crisp. Add olive oil and lemon juice and mix. Serve with a cooked grain or pasta.

Per Serve
Protein 12 g
Calcium 58 mg
Iron 1.5 mg
Wheat, Dairy and Egg-free

TOFU CUTLETS (Serves 3–4)

1 × 400 g block firm tofu
½ cup rice flour
Tamari and water—50% each
Grated ginger—about 1 dsp

Cut the tofu blocks in half—diagonally, and then cut into four layers, making 8 triangles. Marinate in the tamari, water and ginger mixed together. Leave in marinade for 1 hour. Drain triangles and coat in rice flour. Place on an oven tray and bake for 25 minutes at 200°C turning once. Serve on a bed of brown rice, with steamed Asian vegetables and Sweet and Sour Sauce.

Per Serve
Protein 8 g
Calcium 250 mg
Iron 1.4 mg
Wheat, Dairy and Egg-free

TOFU TRIANGLES (Makes 8)

4 sheets filo pastry

Filling:
400 g organic tofu grated
½ cup chopped spring onions
¼ cup chopped coriander leaves
¼ cup grated fresh green ginger
1 dsp tamari
1 clove garlic crushed
1 cup carrot grated
½ cup green peas
½ cup rice flour
½ cup soaked arame chopped
1 egg lightly beaten (optional)

Preheat oven to 180°C. Mix all ingredients together, except egg. Lay two sheets filo together, cut into 4 oblongs. Repeat with the other 2 sheets or line a pie plate with the two sheets. Divide mixture into 8 and place one portion on each oblong, roll up into triangles and place on a greased tray. Brush with egg. Or pile all mixture into lined pie plate and top with 2 sheets filo, brushing base edge with egg before adding top sheets. Pinch edges together and brush top with egg. Prick top with fork or cut several slits. Bake approximately 30 minutes at 180°C.

Per Serve
Protein 7 g
Calcium 66 mg
Iron 2 mg
Dairy-free

Salads

ARAME SALAD (Serves 2)

1 cup soaked arame seaweed
1 cup mushrooms sliced
½ cup carrots thinly sliced

2 spring onions chopped
½ red capsicum thinly sliced
1 tbs Braggs bouillon
3 tbs flaxseed oil dressing

Drain the arame and prepare the vege-tables. Mix gently together with the dressing and Braggs.

Per Serve
Protein 4.75 g
Calcium 55 mg
Iron 4.25 mg
Wheat, Dairy and Egg-free

ASPARAGUS ROLLS (Serves 4)

1 × 425 g can asparagus spears (approx 20–22 spears)
Required amount of sliced wholewheat bread or bread of choice (20 slices)
1 × 105 g can salmon or tuna (optional)
Soy mayonnaise or spread of choice

Drain asparagus and fish. Mash fish with mayonnaise. Cut the crusts from the bread slices and roll each slice with a rolling pin to make thin and easier to roll up, spread with the mayonnaise. Lay 1 asparagus spear diagonally across the slice and roll up firmly. Secure with a toothpick. Can be served as is or in layers in a casserole dish. Cover and heat in the oven. If hot, serve with a cheese sauce and a sprinkle of parsley. Allow 4–5 rolls per person. A good lunch dish. For main meal serve with salad.

Per Serve
Protein 34 g (with fish)
Calcium 273 mg
Iron 0.29 mg
Dairy and Egg-free

BEAN SPROUT SALAD (Serves 4–6)

4 cups mung bean sprouts (blanched)
1 cup carrots shredded
1 cup cabbage shredded
½ cup soaked hijiki chopped
3 cups mushrooms sliced
1 cup celery sliced
1 cup spring onions sliced
1 cup almonds
1½ cup ginger almond sauce

Combine all prepared vegetables and stir sauce through.

Ginger Almond Sauce:
3 tbs almond butter
4 tbs lemon juice
1 tbs tamari
2 tbs grated fresh ginger
1 tbs flax oil
2 tsp honey

Blend sauce ingredients until smooth and creamy.

Per Serve
Protein 13 g
Calcium 171 mg
Iron 3 mg
Wheat, Dairy and Egg-free

CAESAR SALAD

½ cup dried lima beans
¼ cup almonds
¼ small cos lettuce
8 large cherry tomatoes
1 small Lebanese cucumber
½ small bunch asparagus
½ small avocado
1 stick celery

Soak almonds and lima beans overnight separately. Cook lima beans in boiling water until tender. Rinse, drain and refrigerate. Cook asparagus spears in boiling water for 8 minutes. Rinse in cold water and drain. When cool, chop into small pieces.

Pesto:
¼ cup soy mayonnaise
½ cup chopped fresh herbs (thyme, sage, parsley, oregano and basil)
1 tbs crushed garlic

Mix herbs, garlic and mayonnaise together either by hand or with a food wand or processor.

Herb Damper:
1 cup spelt flour
2 tsp baking powder
¼ cup plain yoghurt
¼ cup soy, rice or oat milk
¼ tsp Herbamare
2 tbs chopped fresh herbs

Sift flour and baking powder into a bowl. Add seasonings. Make a well in the centre and pour in the yoghurt and milk. Mix gently to a soft dough and turn onto a greased tray. Press out to 2 cm thickness. Bake in a hot oven for 15 minutes or until golden brown.

Tamari Dressing:
¼ cup flaxseed oil
2 tbs tamari
¼ cup lemon juice

Combine flaxseed oil, tamari and lemon juice in a jar and shake or blend with a food wand or processor. Cut cherry tomatoes in half, wash and tear lettuce, cut cucumbers into bite size pieces. Spread damper with pesto and cut into crouton size pieces. Arrange salad ingredients on a bed of lettuce in a bowl. Top with herb damper croutons and serve with tamari dressing.

Per Serve
Protein 5 g
Calcium 37 mg
Iron 2 mg
Wheat, Dairy and Egg-free

CHICKPEA SALAD (Serves 4)

2 cups cooked chickpeas
1 cup cooked rice
1 large avocado peeled and cut into chunks
1 bunch English spinach washed and torn

Dressing:
2 tbs lemon juice
3 tbs flaxseed oil

½ tsp crushed garlic

½ red capsicum finely chopped

2 tsp chopped fresh oregano

2 ripe tomatoes finely chopped

Mix all together and pour over the salad.

Per Serve
Protein 18.5 g
Calcium 219 mg
Iron 1 mg
Wheat, Dairy and Egg-free

COLD NOODLE SALAD (Serves 3–4)

1 cup green beans sliced

1 cup broccoli florets

1 cup fresh asparagus pieces

2 cups pasta or noodles of choice

2 spring onions chopped

Steam vegetables till just tender, cool. Boil pasta and cool, add the 2 chopped spring onions.

Dressing:
½ cup basic french dressing
Add 2 tsp fresh chopped tarragon
2 tsp lemon juice

Gently fold dressing through vegetables and pasta.

Per Serve
Protein 2 g
Calcium 15 mg
Iron .5 mg
Wheat, Dairy and Egg-free

PRETTY COLESLAW (Serves 4)

2 cups green cabbage sliced

2 cups red cabbage sliced

1 cup carrot grated

1 cup sweet corn kernels

1 cup red capsicum diced

Dressing:

Avocado with lime or lemon

½ avocado mashed

2 tbs cider vinegar

¼ cup lime juice

2 tsp pressed garlic

3 tbs soy mayonnaise

½ cup water

1 tsp soy sauce

Blend all dressing ingredients together in a food processor or with a food wand. Toss through coleslaw vegetables.

Per Serve
Protein 5 g
Calcium 40 mg
Iron 4 mg
Wheat and Dairy-free

FENNEL COLESLAW (Serves 4)

2 small zucchini

2 yellow squash

2 carrots

1 fennel bulb

3 cups cabbage shredded

2 tbs fresh dill chopped

Dressing of choice

Thinly slice zucchini and carrots, julienne the squash, finely shred the cabbage and fennel. Fold dressing through the vegetables.

Per Serve
Protein 1.85 g
Calcium 45 mg
Iron 1 mg
Wheat, Dairy and Egg-free

HIJIKI SALAD (Serves 2)

1 cup hijiki soaked and chopped
½ cup water and 1 tsp tamari
2 tbs lemon juice
1½ cups carrot grated
½ red onion chopped

Sauté hijiki in water and tamari for 10 minutes, allow to cool then mix all ingredients together. Serve on bed of greens.

Per Serve
Protein 4.5 g
Calcium 66 mg
Iron 3 mg
Wheat, Dairy and Egg-free

HOT NOODLE SALAD (Serves 3–4)

1 cup carrots chopped
1 cup snow peas sliced
1 cup red capsicum
1 cup spring onion
1 cup cabbage chopped
2 tbs ginger root grated
1 tbs barley miso dissolved in ½ cup of water

2 cup cooked noodles or pasta of choice
1 cup almonds chopped

Boil or steam vegetables, drain; if boiled, add to hot cooked noodles with ginger, garlic and barley miso. Mix well and serve garnished with chopped almonds.

Per Serve
Protein 9 g
Calcium 96 mg
Iron 1.5 mg
Wheat, Dairy and Egg-free

LENTIL SALAD (Serves 4–6)

1½ cups brown or green lentils
1 cup brown onions chopped
1 cup capsicum chopped
1 cup celery chopped
1 cup red onion chopped
1 tsp garlic
4 cups water

Combine lentils, garlic, brown onion and water in a saucepan, cover and bring to the boil and simmer for 30–40 minutes till soft but not mushy. Combine the other ingredients in a bowl and add drained lentils while hot. Allow to stand for 5 minutes before serving. Serve with a dollop of plain yoghurt.

Per Serve
Protein 25 g
Calcium 98 mg
Iron 3.6 mg
Wheat and Egg-free

MEXICAN PASTA SALAD (HOT OR COLD) (Serves 4–6)

500 g short chunky pasta of choice
1 cup of corn kernels
3 spring onions chopped
1 cup capsicum chopped
1½ cups cooked beans of choice (legumes)
1 cup tomatoes chopped
½ cup black olives sliced
2 tsp ground cumin
2 tbs chopped fresh coriander
¼ cup lemon juice

Cook pasta in boiling water according to packet instructions, add corn for last 3 minutes. If serving salad cold, drain pasta and rinse under cold running water. Mix all ingredients together, serve on a bed of greens. If planning to serve warm, heat on stove or in a covered casserole dish in oven.

Per Serve
Protein 9.5 g
Calcium 282 mg
Iron 4 mg
Wheat, Dairy and Egg-free

NOODLE VEGETABLE SALAD (Serves 4)

1 × 375 pkt hokkein noodles, cooked and drained
2 carrots cut in matchsticks
1 broccoli head sliced
1 cup green beans sliced
1 bunch baby bok-choy washed and trimmed and cut in quarters
150 g soaked shiitake mushrooms sliced
60 g bean sprouts
¼ cup chopped coriander

Place noodles in a large bowl. Heat 2 tbs water in a large pan or wok; add carrots, beans and broccoli, cook for 5 minutes. Add bok-choy, cook for 1 minute, add mushrooms and bean sprouts and coriander, toss gently and add noodles, heat through for about 2–3 minutes, add dressing and serve.

Dressing:
½ cup lemon or lime juice
¼ cup homemade mirin
1 tbs tamari

Per Serve
Protein 5 g
Calcium 70 mg
Iron 1.5 mg
Dairy and Egg-free

WARM POTATO SALAD WITH YOGHURT DRESSING (Serves 4)

1 kg small pontiac potatoes (unpeeled and quartered)
200 g green beans cut in 3 cm lengths
250 g cherry tomatoes halved
½ cup pitted black olives halved
3 spring onions sliced diagonally
1 tsp chopped garlic

Sauté the garlic and potatoes in 2 tbs oil and 2 tbs water. When coated with garlic, cover and cook gently for 20 minutes. Add the beans and cook for another 5 minutes. Mix in remaining ingredients. Serve with dressing.

Yoghurt Dressing:
½ cup soy yoghurt
1 tsp tamari
¼ cup flaxseed oil
½ cup chopped basil

Gradually stir basil into the oil, and then stir in the soy yoghurt and tamari.

Per Serve
Protein 4 g
Calcium 82 mg
Iron 2.5 mg
Wheat, Dairy and Egg-free

RED CABBAGE SALAD
(Serves 4)

¼ head of red cabbage grated
1 beetroot grated
1 cup small green peas
Dressing of lemon juice, honey and garlic

Toss all together and chill.

Per Serve
Protein 4 g
Calcium 32 mg
Iron 3 mg
Wheat, Dairy and Egg-free

RICE PAPER SALAD ROLLS
(Serves 4)

12 sheets rice paper approximately 20 cm diameter
6 cups cabbage, red or green shredded
1 cup fresh mint chopped
½ cup fat-free French dressing
4 cups lettuce shredded
2 cups red capsicum julienned
2 cups snow peas sliced
1 punnet alfalfa sprouts
150 g tofu

Cut tofu in 12 strips, marinate in ½ cup tamari and ½ cup water for 30 minutes. Lightly steam cabbage, rinse and cool and add dressing and mint. Soak rice paper sheets, one at a time in a bowl of warm water until soft and pliable. Work to finish each roll one at a time. Lay one rice paper sheet on a clean tea towel; layer ¹⁄₁₂ of each ingredient in the centre of the rice sheet. Roll up, tucking in the ends as you roll. Serve with a dipping sauce of choice. Fillings can be varied to suit taste. Lettuce leaves can also be used this way. Just wash and lay one or two leaves flat and put fillings in the centre and roll up.

Per Serve
Protein 9 g
Calcium 147 mg
Iron 16 mg
Wheat, Dairy and Egg-free

SEA VEGETABLE SALAD
(Serves 2)

1 cup dried wakame sliced
1 cup arame roughly chopped
4–6 shiitake mushrooms (dried)
2 cups cucumber chopped
1 cup sliced yellow or green capsicum
1 large tomato diced

Dressing:
2 tbs vinegar
½ tsp crushed garlic
2 tsp tamari or soy sauce
1 tbs flax oil

Soak sea vegetables and mushrooms in warm water for 15–20 minutes. Strain off soak water, slice mushrooms. Mix all ingredients together and chill.

Per Serve
Protein 5 g
Calcium 270 mg
Iron 2 mg
Wheat, Dairy and Egg-free

SIMPLE BEETROOT SALAD
(Serves 4)

4 beetroots
3 tbs lemon juice or brown rice vinegar
1 tbs fresh dill chopped
½ cup green peas

Grate beetroot finely, add the other ingredients. Serve with a green salad.

Wheat, Dairy and Egg-free

SPINACH AND PUMPKIN SALAD
(Serves 4)

2 cups large pumpkin peeled and diced
2 cups Jerusalem artichokes or potatoes peeled and dice large
150 g small fresh spinach leaves
2 cups sweet corn kernels
1 cup cooked green peas (fresh is best)
1 lettuce heart
½ bunch parsley
6 tbs olive or flax oil
3 tbs apple cider vinegar

Boil the potato and pumpkin until tender. Wash the spinach and lettuce well. Drain and cool the cooked vegetables. Chop the parsley roughly. Mix the oil and vinegar together. Mix all vegetables together except greens. Arrange the greens on the plates, pile the other vegetables together on the greens. Pour over dressing.

Per Serve
Protein 10 g
Calcium 57 mg
Iron 10 mg
Wheat, Dairy and Egg-free

SPINACH SALAD WITH RICE FLAKES (Serves 4)

3 tbs rice flakes
3 tbs oat flakes
1 zucchini
1 carrot
4 packed cups small spinach leaves

5 red radishes

Dressing:

2 tsp mustard

Juice of 1 lemon

3 tbs soy yoghurt

½ cup flaxseed oil

Soak the rice and oat flakes in boiling water for 5 minutes, then drain. Prepare the dressing and mix together well. Stir 2 tbs dressing into the drained flakes, let stand for 20 minutes. Cut the carrot and zucchini into matchsticks. Shred the spinach finely. Mix vegetables together, serve with the cereals and top with the dressing.

Per Serve

Protein 2 g

Calcium 40 mg

Iron 1 mg

Wheat, Dairy and Egg-free

SPRING SALAD (Serves 4)

1 cup barley

1 carrot

½ cup black olives

1 cup alfalfa sprouts

1 head radicchio

½ tsp ground allspice

Few sprigs fennel

1 clove garlic

Juice of 1 lemon

2 tbs flaxseed oil

Rinse the barley to remove excess starch. Cook barley in boiling water till tender, approximately 1 hour. Drain and rinse under cold water. Prepare the vegetables. Grate the carrot, tear the lettuce, and chop the garlic cloves and fennel. Place the vegetables with the barley in a bowl. Make a dressing with the garlic, lemon and flaxseed oil. Toss all together gently.

Per Serve

Protein 5 g

Calcium 29 mg

Iron 1.6 mg

Wheat, Dairy and Egg-free

SUSHI RICE SALAD (Serves 4)

1 cup brown rice cooked in 3 cups water

2 small carrots, 1 small cucumber, 1 red capsicum diced and steamed

1 sheet nori crumbled

½ cup chopped onion

½ cup chopped almonds

Combine cooked rice and steamed vegetables.

Dressing:

½ cup apple cider vinegar

1 tsp honey

½ tsp Herbamare

2 tsp grated fresh ginger root

Place dressing ingredients in saucepan and simmer for 5 minutes. Cool. Mix salad ingredients and dressing together, serve on a bed of washed salad greens, top with crumbled nori and almonds.

Per Serve
Protein 2.1 g
Calcium 31.5 mg
Iron 1 mg
Wheat, Dairy and Egg-free

SWEET POTATO SALAD
(Serves 4)

3 cups sweet potato—2 cm dice
½ cup chopped arame
¾ cup soy mayonnaise

Scrub sweet potato and dice. Steam until just soft. Soak arame in warm water for 30 minutes. Mix the potato and arame together with the soy mayonnaise. Serve while still warm.

Per Serve
Protein 4 g
Calcium 103 mg
Iron 2.5 mg
Wheat, Dairy and Egg-free

TUNA PASTA SALAD (Serves 4)

300 g dried pasta spirals
1 × 425 g can tuna in spring water
2 cups cooked chickpeas
2 tbs capers drained
1 red onion thinly sliced
2 ripe tomatoes chopped
½ cup chopped parsley

Dressing:
2 tbs lemon juice
1 tsp Dijon mustard
½ cup flaxseed oil

Cook the pasta following packet directions, rinse and cool. Mix dressing together well. Break drained tuna into chunks. Add to vegetables and mix dressing in gently.

Per Serve
Protein 41.5 g
Calcium 197 mg
Iron 7.5 mg
Wheat, Dairy and Egg-free

WARM ORIENTAL VEGETABLE SALAD (Serves 4)

200 g long grain brown rice
6 leaves Chinese cabbage
1 zucchini
50 g daiken (Japanese white radish)
125 g green beans
2 sticks celery
1 carrot
2 large tomatoes
2 spring onions
2 cloves garlic
1 bunch coriander
1 tbs tamari
½ cup flaxseed oil dressing

Cook the rice in boiling water for 20 minutes then drain. Place the cabbage leaves in the bottom of a steamer basket then place the rice on top followed by the diced vegetables. Put a few stalks of coriander in the steamer water and cook vegetables covered for 20–25 minutes. When almost cooked add the chopped tomatoes and coriander, place the lid on and allow to stand a little before serving. Mix the tamari with the dressing and pour over the food when serving.

Per Serve
Protein 2.5 g
Calcium 50 mg
Iron 1.5 mg
Saturated Fat .5 g
Wheat, Dairy and Egg-free

WARM POTATO SALAD (2) (Serves 4)

1 kg small red potatoes (Pontiac) skinned
2 cups green beans halved
1 punnet cherry tomatoes
4 spring onions

Cut potatoes into large dice. Cut beans into approximately 4 cm lengths. Halve cherry tomatoes. Clean and slice spring onions. Steam potatoes and beans. Add tomatoes and onions. Place in a bowl and stir dressing through or pour over when served.

Dressing:
¾ cup packed basil leaves
½ cup nutritional yeast flakes
½ cup plain yoghurt
½ cup nuts of choice
¼ cup olive or flaxseed oil

In a food processor, pulse-chop the nuts and basil. Gradually add the oil and remove from processor and stir in the yoghurt and yeast.

Per Serve
Protein 4 g
Calcium 40 mg
Iron 2 mg
Wheat and Egg-free

WARM TUNA SALAD (Serves 4)

1 pkt (250 g) rice pasta spirals
1 × 425 g can tuna (or salmon)
1 × 400 g can chickpeas
1 red onion sliced thinly
3 tomatoes or 12 cherry tomatoes
2 tbs French dressing
2 tbs chopped parsley

Cook pasta according to packet directions. Drain tuna and chickpeas. Slice tomatoes or cut cherry tomatoes in half. Sauté onion, chickpeas and tomotoes in water for 5 minutes. Mix all ingredients together gently.

Per Serve
Protein 50 g
Calcium 160 mg
Iron 8 mg
Wheat, Dairy and Egg-free

ZUCCHINI AND PASTA SALAD (Serves 4)

1 large zucchini
1 carrot
1 small fennel bulb
4 spring onions
200 g broccoli
1 cup cooked peas
2½ cups pasta of choice

1 cup cooked beetroot diced
2 tomatoes diced
1 red onion chopped finely
Small bunch lemon balm roughly chopped
1 tbs cider vinegar
1 tbs lemon juice

Wash and chop up the vegetables. Steam vegetables except tomatoes, red onion and herbs. Rinse vegetables under cold running water. Cook pasta according to packet instructions. Gently fold all ingredients together.

Per Serve
Protein 4.6 g
Calcium 86 mg
Iron 4 mg
Wheat, Dairy and Egg-free

Soups

BEAN SOUP (Serves 4)

10 cm stick wakame
½ cup dried Lima beans (soaked overnight = 1 cup)
½ onion chopped
1 cup carrots chopped
5 cups water
1 dsp miso dissolved in ½ cup warm water

Drain lima beans and discard soak water. Cook lima beans and wakame in the 5 cups of fresh water, add carrots and onions and cook until tender. Can be pureed. Add dissolved miso.

Per Serve
Protein 6 g
Calcium 57 mg
Iron 1 mg
Wheat, Dairy and Egg-free

BROCCOLI AND ALMOND SOUP (Serves 4)

4 cups broccoli roughly chopped
1 onion chopped
2 tbs almonds chopped
4 cups water
½ cup soy milk
1 tsp mineral bouillon or 1 vegetable stock cube

Chop onion, put into pan with water. Bring water to the boil and add broccoli including chopped stalk. Cook until soft. Add bouillon and soy milk. Puree. Just before serving, add almonds.

Per Serve
Protein 8 g
Calcium 106 mg
Iron 2 mg
Wheat, Dairy and Egg-free

CARROT AND CAULIFLOWER SOUP (Serves 4)

1 small onion chopped
1 tsp garlic crushed
2 dsp mild curry powder
2 large carrots chopped
1 cauliflower chopped into small pieces
1–2 cups soy milk

2 tbs mineral bouillon
1 tsp Herbamare

Chop onion; sauté in a small amount of water with the garlic. Add the curry powder. Cook until onion is soft and then add carrots and cauliflower. Cover with water and simmer until carrot is tender. Add the mineral bouillon and ½ teaspoon of Herbamare. Use a food wand or processor to mix to a good soup consistency. Add 1–2 cups of soy milk. Do not boil after adding the soy milk or soup may curdle.

Per Serve
Protein 4 g
Calcium 65 mg
Iron 1.6 mg
Wheat, Dairy and Egg-free

CAULIFLOWER SOUP (Serves 4)

6 cups cauliflower roughly chopped
3 onion diced
1 tsp cumin powder
1 cup soy milk or milk of choice

Cook onion and cauliflower in enough water to cover well, cook until soft. Blend, add in cumin and soy milk. Reheat but do not boil. Serve with chopped parsley.

Per Serve
Protein 4.5 g
Calcium 51 mg
Iron 1.5 mg
Wheat, Dairy and Egg-free

CELERY SOUP (Serves 4)

1 chopped onion
½–1 bunch of celery (approx. 8 cups chopped)
1 litre of soy milk
2 tbs Braggs mineral bouillon or 2 vegetable stock cubes
Ground fennel seeds
Ground celery seeds
Pinch mixed spice
Herbamare to taste

Chop onion, sauté in a small amount of water. Cook until onion is soft. Then add celery. Add minimal water (2 cups) and simmer until celery is tender. Add the Braggs mineral bouillon and ½ teaspoon of Herbamare and herbs and spices. Purée. Add soy milk and re-heat. Do not boil after adding the soy milk or soup may curdle.

Per Serve
Protein 11.5 g
Calcium 161 mg
Iron 9 mg
Wheat, Dairy and Egg-free

CORN DUMPLINGS (Makes 15)

1 cup cornmeal (polenta)
1 cup spelt, wholemeal or cornflour
½ tsp Herbamare
½–1 cup boiling water

Mix cornmeal and flour and the Herbamare. Add enough of the water to mix to a soft dough. Knead for 5 minutes, when the dough is stiff and smooth, pinch off small pieces and shape into balls. Drop all together in boiling water or a broth and boil for 30 minutes. Serve in a soup or with vegetables or beans.

CURRIED ZUCCHINI SOUP (Serves 4)

2 large zucchini (approximately 8–10 cups chopped)
2 onions
1 tbs bouillon
½ tbs curry powder
1 cup soy milk

Chop onions and zucchini, cover with water and cook, with curry powder, until soft, then puree. Add soy milk and bouillon to taste. Garnish with finely chopped red capsicum.

Per Serve
Protein 4 g
Calcium 25 mg
Iron 2 mg
Wheat, Dairy and Egg-free

GREEN SOUP (Serves 2)

½ cup tofu diced
2 cups mixed greens chopped
3 cups water and 1 tsp vegetable powder or 1 cube
1 dsp arrowroot or kuzu dissolved in 2 tbs water
¼ tsp Herbamare

Sauté in a little water or steam tofu for 5 minutes, add Herbamare. Add chopped greens, sauté for 2 minutes. Add stock and simmer till greens are bright green, add thickening mix and simmer till thickened. Puree and serve topped with yoghurt.

GREEN TOFU SOUP (Serves 4)

1½ litres water
2 vegetable cubes or 1 tsp vegetable powder
375 g spinach, washed and roughly chopped
200 g tofu diced small
1 tsp grated ginger root
1½ tbs tamari
1 cup of dried cubed bread (for garnish)

Dissolve vegetable cube or powder in water, add all other ingredients except cubed bread. Boil for 15 minutes then puree. Top with croutons and chopped parsley.

Per Serve
Protein 8 g
Calcium 230 mg
Iron 4 mg
Wheat, Dairy and Egg-free

LENTIL SOUP (1) (Serves 4)

500 g brown lentils (soaked for 2 hours and strained)
2 litres water
2 onions chopped

1 potato
1 carrot
2 stalks celery
2 tomatoes
2 cloves garlic
½ tsp sea salt

Dice all vegetables. Place in a pot with the lentils and water. Bring to the boil and simmer for 30 minutes.

Per Serve
Protein 24 g
Calcium 70 mg
Iron 7 mg
Wheat, Dairy and Egg-free

LENTIL SOUP (2)

1 cup dried brown lentils
4 cups water
1 medium onion, chopped
1 medium red capsicum, chopped
3 cups chopped tomatoes
2 cups corn (cut off the cob)
2 large cloves garlic, minced
1 tsp basil
1 tsp mixed herbs
3 tbs tamari (soy sauce)
Parsley

Wash lentils and cook in the four cups of water until soft (30–40 minutes). Add all the vegetables, tomatoes, herbs and tamari, simmer for about 20 minutes until all vegetables are tender. When serving sprinkle with parsley and offer crusty wholemeal bread or rolls. This is a complete meal on its own.

Wheat, Dairy and Egg free (when not served with bread). Rich in Protein, Calcium and Iron.

MISO SOUP BASE (Serves 3)

1 stick washed Kombu
1 cup carrots diced
6 cups cold water
1 cup cabbage diced
2 small onions chopped
1 tbs grated green ginger
1 tbs barley miso
4 spring onions chopped
1 cup celery sliced

Simmer the Kombu, onions, carrots, cabbage and celery in water for 30 minutes. Take out the Kombu and chop finely. Return to pot with miso dissolved in ½ cup warm water and ginger. Mix but don't boil. Serve with spring onions on top.

Per Serve
Protein 2 g
Calcium 72 mg
Iron 2.5 mg

Traditional Additions:
1 cup tofu diced
½ cup sliced shiitake mushrooms
½ sheet nori shredded (add when serving)

Per Serve
Protein 5 g
Calcium 23 mg
Iron 0.5 mg
Wheat, Dairy and Egg-free

NOODLE SOUP (Serves 4)

½ tsp seven spice
1 tsp celery seed
200 g dried rice noodles
200 g snow peas sliced diagonally
200 g bean sprouts
2 carrots cut into thin sticks
1 litre water

Heat 2 tbs water or 1 tbs water and 1 tbs olive oil. Sauté seeds and spices for 2 minutes, stirring constantly. Stir in the water, add rice noodles, snow peas, sprouts and carrots and cook for 1 minute. Serve with chopped parsley and warm pita bread.

Per Serve
Protein 7.5 g
Calcium 34.5 mg
Iron 1.6 mg
Wheat, Dairy and Egg-free

PARSNIP AND LEEK SOUP
(Serves 6)

1 kg parsnips
2 large leeks
1 large onion
1 large potato
1 tsp crushed garlic
2 stalks celery
1½ litres water
½ tsp thyme, oregano, coriander or cumin
Pinch of paprika

Bring water to boil, add vegetables—coarsely chopped. Then add herbs and spices. Simmer until cooked, blend. Add soy milk if too thick.

Per Serve
Protein 24 g
Calcium 122 mg
Iron 4 mg
Saturated Fat 5 g
Wheat, Dairy and Egg-free

ROOT VEGETABLE SOUP
(Serves 3–4)

½ cup oatmeal
6 cups water
1 sliced leek
1 turnip or swede diced
1 large carrot diced
1 dsp tamari

Cook oats in water for 10 minutes then puree. Sauté vegetables in a little water then add vegetables to the oat mixture, simmer for 15 minutes, puree if desired.

Per Serve
Protein 1.5 g
Calcium 30 mg
Iron 1.5 mg
Wheat, Dairy and Egg-free

SIMPLE MINESTRONE SOUP
(Serves 4)

2½ litres water with 4–6 vegetable cubes dissolved in it
1 cup carrots diced
1 cup celery diced
1 cup tomatoes diced
1 cup green beans diced
2 cups shell noodles (rice)
½ tsp sea salt

Place all ingredients except noodles in a saucepan and boil for 20 minutes, stirring occasionally. Add noodles for the last 10 minutes. Serve with garlic bread.

Per Serve
Protein 3 g
Calcium 40 mg
Iron 3 mg
Wheat, Dairy and Egg-free

SPECIAL SPINACH SOUP
(Serves 4)

1 large bunch spinach
½ litre water
1 medium onion chopped
2 tbs plain flour of choice
½ tsp sea salt
1 tbs lemon juice

1 litre water with 2 bouillon cubes dissolved in water
1 hard-boiled egg
2 tbs plain yoghurt

Wash spinach and cook 10 minutes in the ½ litre water. Drain and reserve liquid, adding it to the 1 litre water and cubes. Sauté chopped onion in a little water, add flour and keep stirring. Gradually pour in the 1½ litres of liquid. Bring to the boil and simmer 10 minutes. Chop the spinach very finely and add into the soup along with the lemon juice and sea salt, if needed. Heat gently. Serve with a slice of egg and a dollop of yoghurt on top.

Per Serve
Protein 2 g
Calcium 40 mg
Iron 1 mg
Saturated Fat 1 g

SPICY TOMATO SOUP (Serves 4)

1½ cups dried pasta
1 onion chopped finely
2 × 400 g cans of organic Italian tomatoes diced
1 tbs curry powder
1 tsp ground cardamom
1 tsp ground cinnamon
¼ tsp ground cloves
2 cups vegetable stock (2 vegetable cubes)
Chopped fresh coriander and crusty bread to serve

Cook the pasta and keep warm. Sauté the spices in a little water till aromatic. Add tomatoes and stock bring to the boil then simmer for 5 minutes, puree lightly. Stir in the desired pasta and heat through. Add coriander when serving, with hot bread rolls.

Per Serve
Protein 2.5 g
Calcium 50 mg
Iron 1.25 mg
Wheat, Dairy and Egg-free

SWEET POTATO SOUP
(Serves 4)

1½ litre water
3 vegetable cubes or 1 dsp vegetable seasoning
4 cups small sweet potato diced
1 leak or 2 onions sliced
½ cup celery diced
½ cup carrot diced
2 tsp fresh chopped rosemary

Place all together in saucepan, bring to the boil, simmer until potatoes are tender, then puree.

Per Serve
Protein 1.5 g
Calcium 132 mg
Iron 1 mg
Wheat, Dairy and Egg-free

Dressings

COLESLAW DRESSING
(Makes 2 cups)

1 medium avocado
2 cloves garlic
¼ cup chopped celery leaves
¼ cup lemon juice
1 tbs Braggs liquid aminos
½ dsp cumin
1¼ cups water

Blend in a processor until well pureed.

FLAX OIL DRESSING

5 tbs flaxseed oil (cold extracted)
1 small clove garlic crushed
½ tsp mustard
3 tbs apple cider vinegar
½ tsp honey

Combine all the ingredients well (a food wand or processor works best). Store in refrigerator. This is a base dressing recipe. Contains a good quantity of omega 3. To this can be added almost any other flavour such as:
—chopped sundried tomato and olives
—avocado pureed
—any pureed vegetable or legume
—soy mayonnaise
—any herbs or extra garlic.

GARLIC VINAIGRETTE

¼ cup water
⅓ cup lemon juice
⅓ cup flaxseed oil
3 garlic cloves
5 basil leaves
1 tsp Braggs liquid aminos

Blend well.

HONEY MUSTARD DRESSING
(Makes 1 cup)

For salad greens or cooked greens.

2 heads roasted garlic
2 tbs Dijon mustard
1½ tbs honey
3 tbs cider vinegar
¼ cup apple juice
½ tsp Herbamare

Squeeze the paste from the roasted heads of garlic, place all the ingredients into the bowl of a food processor or puree with a food wand.

MINT YOGHURT DRESSING
(Makes 1 cup)

Serve as dip or on salad or vegetables. Good on potato salad.

1 cup yoghurt
2 tsp finely chopped spring onion or red onion

1 tbs finely chopped fresh dill
1 tbs finely chopped fresh mint
½ tsp garlic
2 tsp lemon juice
¼ tsp Herbamare

Mix all together, let stand for ½ hour before serving.

TOFU MAYONNAISE
(Makes 2 cups)

1½ cups small diced tofu
½ cup soy yoghurt
1 tbs lemon juice
1 tbs tamari
2 tbs flaxseed oil
½ tsp crushed garlic
¼ tsp Herbamare

Process in food blender or mix together with a food wand. Use on salad or hot vegetables.

Protein 19 g
Calcium 622 mg
Iron 9 mg
Wheat, Dairy and Egg-free

TOMATO BASIL DRESSING
(Makes 1 cup)

6 sundried tomatoes
1 cup chopped fresh tomato
½ tsp garlic
¼ cup chopped fresh basil

¼ cup water
2 tbs vinegar (cider or balsamic)
¼ tsp Herbamare

Finely chop sundried tomatoes then puree all ingredients together. Good for pasta-type salads.

Sauces

CURRIED YOGHURT SAUCE
(Serves 4)

½ cup water
1 onion diced small
1 tsp curry powder
1½–2 cups soy yoghurt
3 tsp cornflour dissolved in ¼ cup cold water

Sauté onion in water. Add curry powder. Cook for 3 minutes. Add yoghurt and heat gently, if too thin add cornflour and boil for 1 minute. Pour sauce over hot vegetables and diced marinated tofu.

Per Serve
Protein 8 g
Calcium 152 mg
Iron 1 mg
Saturated Fat 2.5 g
Wheat, Dairy and Egg-free

GREEN CHICKPEA PASTA SAUCE
(Serves 4)

2 cups of cooked chickpeas
2 bunches spinach or 1 bunch of silver beet chopped
1 red capsicum chopped roughly
1 onion chopped
2 tbs lemon juice
1 tsp coriander
1 tsp cumin
½ tsp Herbamare

Sauté onions in a little water, add capsicum and cook for 2–3 minutes, add chickpeas and ¼ cup water simmer for 5 minutes, add chopped silver beet stir and cook for 3 minutes, stir in lemon juice and Herbamare. Serve over cooked pasta or rice. Top with yoghurt sauce.

Per Serve
Protein 12.5 g
Calcium 245.5 mg
Iron 7 mg
Wheat, Dairy and Egg-free

PASTA SAUCE

Can also be used over burgers, polenta or pizza.

1 red onion
1 cup carrots chopped
1 stalk celery diced
4 medium beetroot cooked and pureed
2 tbs rice flour

1 tbs tamari
1 tsp crushed garlic
3 cups water
1 tbs chopped parsley

Sauté onion in a little water. Add carrots and celery, then pureed beetroot. Add 1 cup water, bring to the boil then simmer for 20 minutes stirring occasionally. Add rice flour diluted in 2 cups water. Add soy sauce and other seasonings, simmer for another 10 minutes. Serve over pizza, pasta or vegetables and sprinkle with parsley.

Per Serve
Protein 3 g
Calcium 95 mg
Iron 4 mg
Wheat, Dairy and Egg-free

PIZZA SAUCE

2 medium onions diced
2 × 400 g cans pureed tomatoes (or 1 kg chopped fresh tomatoes)
1 small can tomato paste
1 tsp basil
1 tsp oregano
2 tsp crushed garlic
2 tbs tamari or 1 tsp Herbamare

Mix all ingredients in a saucepan and boil for 5 minutes to thicken. Pita breads can be used as a base for pizza. Top with the tomato sauce and any vegetables of choice, raw, grated or lightly steamed. Place topped pizza on a greased tray and heat in oven for 15 minutes at 180°C.

Per Serve
Protein 6 g
Calcium 115 mg
Iron 1 mg

SPROUTED ALMOND SAUCE

1 cup almonds (soaked in 2 cups water)
½ cup water
¼ cup lemon juice
2 tbs Braggs or tamari
1 garlic clove
1 tbs nutritional yeast
¼ tsp curry powder

Soak the almonds for 12–18 hours (increases vitality). Blend almonds in food processor, adding ½ cup water, and then blend in rest of ingredients, serve over vegetables.

YOGHURT SAUCE

¾ cup plain yoghurt
½ tsp crushed garlic
1 tsp chopped mint
dash Herbamare

Mix well together. Good for hot vegetables.

Fish recipes

FISH ROLLS

1 small can tuna or salmon
1 cup cooked rice
2 cups cooked sweet potato
1 cup cooked parsnip
½ cup spring onion
2 sheets low-fat flaky pastry

Mash potatoes and parsnip, drain fish. Mix fish, rice and vegetables together. Roll pastry a little thinner and cut each square into 4. Divide mixture evenly between the 8 squares. Roll up pastry tucking in the ends as you go, diagonally works well. Prick with a fork, put on greased tray and cook for 30 minutes at 200°C.

Per Serve
Protein 10 g
Calcium 41 mg
Iron 4 mg
Dairy and Egg-free

GINGERED FISH (Serves 4)

750 g Deep Sea Fish fillets (4 fillets)
2 carrots
2 bunches baby bok choy
1 tsp crushed garlic
5 cm piece of green ginger
2 tsp fish sauce
1 tsp sugar
1½ cups jasmine rice

Cut the fish fillets in half crossways. Thinly slice the carrots lengthways. Trim the stalks off the bok choy and wash. Grate the green ginger. Cook the rice according to packet directions. Preheat oven to 180°C. Mix the fish sauce, garlic, ginger and sugar in a bowl. Grease baking pan and place ¼ sliced carrot in one corner. Pile on ¼ bok choy. Place 2 pieces of fish on the top and drizzle ¼ of the sauce over. Repeat in each corner. Cover and cook for approximately 25–30 minutes. Uncover and place each fish stack on the bed of rice on each plate. Pour any pan juices over the stacks.

Per Serve
Protein 41 g
Calcium 264 mg
Iron 4 mg
Wheat, Dairy and Egg-free

SALMON OR TUNA PATE

1 cup canned beans (Lima or Cannellini)
2 tbs chopped parsley
2 tbs lemon juice
1 cup salmon or tuna canned

Blend all together and serve on toast.

Per Serve
Protein 74 g
Calcium 132 mg
Iron 8 mg

SALMON SPRING ROLLS

440 g can of salmon (or tuna or cooked fish)
1 packet spring roll wrappers

½ cup carrot juice
1 chopped onion
1 cup cooked brown rice
1 tbs tomato paste
1 tsp chopped garlic

Combine all ingredients and place 2 large spoonfuls into spring roll wrappers and fold up, place in a greased dish and bake in a moderate oven at 180°C till golden brown.

Protein 20 g
Calcium 299 mg
Iron 3 mg
Saturated Fat 1 g
Wheat, Dairy and Egg-free

SALMON AND TOMATO PASTA (Serves 4)

¾ pkt tomato tagliatelle
1 cup soy milk
1 diced onion
1 × 440 g can salmon, preferably red salmon
3 sticks celery sliced
1 capsicum sliced
½ tsp mustard powder
1 tsp cumin
2 heaped tsp cornflour

Cook pasta as directed by packet then drain. Add celery, onion and capsicum to pasta. Stir through pasta. Mix cornflour to a paste with the soy milk and spices, place in a saucepan. Add 2 cups boiling water, heat and stir till boiling. Add flaked salmon, stir thru pasta and vegetables. Can be served as is or reheated in a casserole for 20–25 minutes at 180°C.

Per Serve
Protein 22 g
Calcium 290 mg
Iron 3.5 mg
Saturated Fat 1 g

SALMON SAUCE WITH RICE NOODLES (Serves 4)

3 cups rice pasta
1 × 415 g can red salmon (drain and break up with fork)
1 cup carrots sliced
1 cup red capsicum sliced
½ cup snow peas sliced

Cook rice pasta in boiling water for 8–10 minutes. Drain and rinse under cold running water and set aside. Steam vegetables lightly. Place a pot of water to boil, when boiling add pasta, reheat 30 seconds and drain. Place in bowls, add salmon sauce and then top with steamed vegetables.

Sauce:
½ litre milk
½ red onion finely chopped
2 tbs plain flour
1 tsp Herbamare
2 tbs water
2 tbs chopped parsley

Sauté onion in 2 tbs water for 5 minutes. Add the flour. Cook, stirring for several minutes gradually pouring in milk, stirring constantly to remove any lumps. Boil for 1 minute. Add Herbamare, salmon and parsley.

Per Serve
Protein 28 g
Calcium 320 mg
Iron 3 mg

TUNA CASSEROLE (Serves 4)

1 × 425 g can tuna, no salt
3 medium potatoes sliced and steamed
1 red onion finely chopped
1 cup sweetcorn kernels
1 cup chopped celery
½ tsp Herbamare
1 cup white sauce

Add corn and vegetables to hot sauce, arrange layers of tuna, vegetables and potatoes, sprinkle with chopped parsley and bake in oven 180°C for 30 minutes.

Per Serve
Protein 10 g
Calcium 278 mg
Iron 6 mg
Wheat, Dairy and Egg-free

TUNA STIR-FRY

1 × 412 g can tuna
1 tbs lemon juice
2 onions diced
1 red capsicum chopped
2 cups cabbage finely sliced
1 cup cauliflower pieces
2 cups zucchini sliced
1 cup broccoli pieces
1 tsp chopped garlic
1 tbs tamari
1 cup water or stock
1 dsp cornflour

Sauté onion, garlic and capsicum in a little water and tamari, add all the vegetables and 1 cup water or stock, and lemon juice. Steam covered for 10 minutes, add tuna. Mix cornflour with a little water and add to the liquid in the fry pan, stir gently till boiling, simmer for 1 minute.

Per Serve
Protein 3.5 g
Calcium 90 mg
Iron 5.6 mg
Wheat, Dairy and Egg-free

Bread

FLAKY PIE CRUST

3 cups wholemeal or spelt flour
2 tbs oil or 1 tsp liquid lecithin
½ tsp sea salt
⅔ cup of hot water

Pre-heat the oven to 250°C. Combine dry ingredients. Rub in oil and lecithin. Add hot water slowly. Roll into a ball and cut in half. Roll out 1 piece and line a greased pie plate, add filling, roll out other half and place on top. Prick with a fork and flute the edges. Bake for 40 to 50 minutes.

CHAPATTIS

3 cups spelt flour OR a mix of 1 cup oat, 1 cup rice and 1 cup spelt flour
1 tsp olive oil
½ tsp sea salt or salt substitute
1 cup water

Combine dry ingredients—flour and salt. Mix in water. Knead well, mixture should be spongy and slightly sticky. Allow dough to rest at least 1 hour or better still rest if overnight, covered in a bowl. Lightly flour a board or your bench or table and roll mixture into very thin rounds, the thinner the better.

Heat a fry pan or skillet. Brush each chapatti on each side with the oil but don't oil the pan. Cook chapattis on each side for approximately 1 minute or until light brown. You can also bake at 180 degrees for 15 minutes until golden. Good when served warm.

PIZZA

Bread Base:
Spelt Flour Bread Base

Tomato Sauce:
1 onion chopped
1 × 400 g tinned tomatoes or 4 large chopped tomatoes
1 tsp mixed dried Italian herbs
1 clove crushed garlic

Toppings:
Kalamata olives
1 Capsicum
6 large mushrooms

Sauté onion in water till soft. Add garlic and tomatoes, add herbs. Simmer gently for 30 minutes making sure it does not stick to bottom of pan. Cool. Cut in four, remove seeds and membrane from capsicum and place fat slices of capsicum, skin side up on oven trays. Place in hot oven. Bake for 5–10 minutes till skin is blistered and blackened. Remove from oven and cover with another tray. Allow to cool. When cool, peel and slice. To assemble pizza, place pizza base on oiled oven tray, spread with tomato sauce. Top with mushrooms, capsicums and olives, or toppings of choice. Bake in preheated hot oven for 10–15 minutes or till done. Enjoy!

Protein 3 g
Calcium 61 mg
Iron 3.25 mg
Wheat, Dairy and Egg-free

SAVOURY CORN LOAF

2 cups polenta or 1½ cups polenta and
½ cup spelt flour
3 tsp aluminum-free baking powder
1 egg
1 cup oat or soy milk
1 tbs olive oil
1 tbs gherkin spread or relish
2 tbs chopped sundried tomatoes

Mix dry ingredients together. Mix together all the remaining ingredients. Add the two mixes together stirring only until combined, do not over-mix. Place mixture in 20 cm greased loaf pan and bake at 200°C for approximately 30 minutes. For a variation, omit savoury flavourings and add 2 tbs honey for a sweet loaf.

Protein 39 g
Calcium 49 mg
Iron 9 mg
Wheat and Dairy-free

SPELT BREAD RECIPE FOR BREADMAKER

400 ml water
2 tsp olive oil
½ tsp honey
⅛ tsp Herbamarc or salt
5 cups wholemeal spelt flour
2 tsp instant dried yeast

Set Breadmaker to Wholemeal Setting 750 g loaf. Place ingredients in recom-mended order, usually as listed above, water first then oil etc.

SPELT FLOUR BREAD

6 cups spelt flour
2 cups unbleached white or wholemeal flour
½ tbs dry yeast or 75 g fresh yeast
2 tsp honey
1 litre warm water
1 tbs cold-pressed olive oil

Mix ¾ of the dry ingredients together. Pour in ¾ of the liquid and all the honey. Mix well. Add the remaining flours and liquid, mix well, then let the mixture rest until it doubles in size. When doubled, remove from bowl onto a floured surface and knead for 8–10 minutes. Divide the dough in half and put into two 700 g bread tins. Spray with water and allow to double in size again. Bake at 220°C for 30 minutes.

WALNUT CORNBREAD

1 cup polenta
1 cup wholemeal or spelt flour
1 tbs baking powder
1 tsp carbonate soda
1 tsp cinnamon
1½ cups chopped walnuts
3 bananas
2 tbs honey

2 tsp vanilla essence
½ cup soy milk
¼ cup melted butter or olive oil

Place soy milk, butter, honey, vanilla, essence and 2 bananas in a food processor, process until smooth. Add the sifted dry ingredients, pulse chop until just blended. Transfer to a bowl and stir in the walnuts and the one remaining sliced banana. Pour into a greased pan and bake at 180°C for approximately 50 minutes.

Protein 51 g
Calcium 248 mg
Iron 13.5 mg

Dips, spreads and stuffings

ASPARAGUS GUACAMOLE
(Makes 1½–2 cups)

4–6 asparagus cooked or steamed
1 avocado
2 tbs lemon juice
pinch cayenne
1 tbs red onion or spring onion finely chopped
½ tsp Herbamare or tamari
1 medium tomato diced small

Puree all together except for tomato. Stir in after pureeing.

Per Serve
Protein 4 g
Calcium 115 mg
Iron 11.5 mg
Wheat, Dairy and Egg-free

BEAN GUACAMOLE
(Makes 2 cups)

1 avocado
1½ cups cooked beans or chickpeas
1 cup tomato chopped
1 tsp garlic
1 tsp coriander
½ tsp cumin
2 tsp lemon juice
½ tsp garam masala
½ cup spring onions
Water if needed or 1 tbs oil

Puree chickpeas, add other ingredients puree well. If desired, flavour with Herbamare or tamari. Serve as spread or sauce over vegetable curry.

Protein 27 g
Calcium 45 mg
Iron 17.5 mg
Wheat, Dairy and Egg-free

BEETROOT STUFFING FOR CELERY, PEPPERS OR TOMATOES
(Serves 3–4)

½ cup almonds, soaked in water drained and then ground
1 cup rejuvelac
1 cup dulse

2 medium beetroot finely grated
1 tsp lemon rind grated
1 large garlic clove

Pulse chop the first four ingredients in a food processor and place in a bowl, stir in the rest of the ingredients.

LENTIL SPREAD

½ cup red or green lentils
½ cup chickpeas or lima beans (can use canned)
2 tsp curry powder
2 tsp coriander powder
2 tsp chopped garlic
2 tbs lemon juice
2 tbs Braggs bouillon
½ tsp Herbamare
2 tbs flax oil
Water

Drain chickpeas or tinned beans if canned. If using fresh bring to the boil and simmer until peas are soft. Cover lentils with water and cook until soft. Rinse beans or chick peas and lentils. Puree them in a blender, adding the rest of the ingredients, slowly adding enough water to mix to cream consistency.

Per Serve
Protein 18.5 g
Calcium 101 mg
Iron 5 mg
Wheat, Dairy and Egg-free

LIMA BEAN DIP
(Makes 2½ cups)

3 cups cooked lima beans
½ tsp pressed garlic (2 cloves)
2 tbs fresh lemon juice
2 tbs chopped fresh dill (1 tbs dry)
1 tbs chopped fresh mint (1 dsp dry)
1 tbs flaxseed oil
¼ cup chopped spring onion or red onion
½ tsp Herbamare
If needed add 2 tbs of liquid from the beans or water to puree.

Puree all; serve as a dip or spread.

Per Serve
Protein 12 g
Calcium 96 mg
Iron 6 mg
Wheat, Dairy and Egg-free

PESTO

Handful fresh parsley
Handful fresh basil
2 tbs soy mayonnaise
2 cloves garlic
Dash of lemon juice
Herbamare (to taste)

Blend all ingredients together (use a food processor or blender) to a soft paste consistency.

RAITA

300 g tub of soy yoghurt
½ continental cucumber
2 tsp crushed dill seeds
1 tsp crushed garlic

Cut cucumber in small diced pieces. Thoroughly mix all ingredients together and chill before serving.

SAVOURY CRUMBLE TOPPING

1 cup rolled oats
1 tbs soy mayonnaise
1 dsp tamari
1 tsp mixed herbs

Coarsely grind the oats in a food processor and mix in the herbs. Combine the mayonnaise and tamari, and then add to the oat mix. Use as required.

STUFFING FOR CAPSICUM, GOLDEN NUGGET PUMPKIN OR ZUCCHINI (Makes 6 cups)

2 cups cooked beans of choice (lima or kidney etc.)
½ cup chopped onion
1 cup chopped celery
1 cup chopped capsicum
1 tsp vegetable broth powder
½ cup tomato puree
½ tsp diced sage
1 cup finely chopped almonds
¾ cup finely chopped black olives

Mix all ingredients together and stuff vegetables. Place vegetables in covered baking dish and bake approximately 1 hour at 180°C, removing cover for the last 15 minutes.

SWEET POTATO DIP

1 large sweet potato
1 clove garlic minced
⅓ cup ground almonds
¼ cup lemon juice
1 tbs flaxseed oil

Peel, dice and steam potato until soft then mash. Mix together well with other ingredients. Serve with vegetable sticks.

TOFU DIP

2 cups tofu
1 tbs yeast flakes
2 tsp tamari
½ tsp cumin
1 dsp chopped parsley
1 dsp chopped celery
2 tbs cider vinegar
½ tsp tumeric
1 tbs soy yoghurt

Blend all ingredients together.

Protein 28.4 g
Calcium 446 mg
Iron 5 mg
Wheat, Dairy and Egg-free

TOFU OR TEMPEH AND AVOCADO SPREAD OR DIP

1 avocado
100 g seasoned tempeh or tofu

If using tempeh, crumble and sauté in a pan with a little water (2 tbs) for 10 minutes. Tofu can be used as is. Peel and roughly chop avocado. Place both ingredients in a food processor and process until smooth.

Per Serve
Protein 7 g
Calcium 100 mg
Iron 6 mg

TOFU TOMATO SPREAD
(Serves 4)

1 cup tofu
¼ cup chopped tomato
½ tsp dried basil
½ tsp dried marjoram
¼ tsp Herbamare

Place all ingredients in food processor and blend until smooth. If using fresh herbs, double quantity to 1 teaspoon.

Per Serve
Protein 8.5 g
Calcium 135 mg
Iron 1.5 mg
Wheat, Dairy and Egg-free

TOFU SPREAD

Great for rollups, sandwiches, on toast or pita bread.

200 g seasoned tofu
½ cup capsicum diced
½ cup celery diced
½ cup red onion diced
1 cup chopped parsley
1 tsp dill
1 tsp mustard
1 tsp lemon juice
½ cup mayonnaise

Grate or mash tofu then mix with all other ingredients.

Per Serve
Protein 19.5 g
Calcium 577 mg
Iron 2.2 mg
Wheat, Dairy and Egg-free

Desserts

AGAR AGAR FOR JAM

4 cups cooked, drained and mashed fruit
2 cups of the fruit juice from cooked fruit
5 tbs agar agar
½ cup apple juice concentrate
¼ tsp allspice, cinnamon or cloves (optional)
1 tbs lemon juice

Dissolve agar agar in the juice by boiling gently, constantly stirring. Add the rest of the ingredients, boil 1 minute. Pour into sterilised jars and seal. Refrigerate jam after opening jar otherwise will ferment.

APPLE OAT PIKELETS (Makes 20)

1 cup unbleached flour of choice
⅔ cup rolled oats
2 tsp salt skip or Lotus brand baking powder
2 tsp cinnamon
1 egg lightly beaten
2 tbs honey
1½ cups soy milk or rice or oat milk
½ cup chopped almonds
1 medium apple grated

Sift flour, cinnamon and baking powder. Stir in oats and make a well in centre. Combine honey, egg and milk, then gradually add to flour. Stir in apple and nuts. Cover mixture and stand for 10 minutes. Drop mixture by tablespoon into a lightly greased frying pan. When bubbles appear on top, turn over and cook until lightly browned.

BANANA DESSERT

250 g silken tofu
1 medium ripe banana
1 tbs vanilla
½ cup soy milk
3 dsp arrowroot

Place all ingredients in a saucepan and puree with a food wand or processor.

Place on heat and whisk gently until mixture boils. Simmer 3–4 minutes, stirring gently. Pour into serving glasses or bowls. Decorate with some fresh fruit slices or chopped nuts. Chill for several hours before serving.

BREAD PUDDING

3 cups stale bread cubed
1 cup dried fruit
2 cups apple juice
1 tsp cinnamon
½ tsp cardamom
1 tbs grated lemon grind
½ cup chopped almonds

Soak all ingredients except nuts in the apple juice for 3 hours. Spoon mixture into greased casserole type dish and sprinkle with chopped almonds. Bake covered at 200°C, for 30 minutes uncover and bake until browned on top.

FROZEN FRUIT TREATS

1 block carob or chocolate
bananas, grapes or strawberries

Melt carob or chocolate in a bowl over a pot of boiling water. Dip pieces of banana, grapes or strawberries in the melted carob or chocolate. Place on a greased plate until set. Remove from plate to a tray suitable to go into the freezer and freeze. Note: A nice treat on a hot day. Many fruits are suitable to thread onto wooden skewers and freeze. Large grapes are good for this. Other fruits can be cut to appropriate size and threaded on skewers.

FROZEN YOGHURT TREATS
(Makes 6 popsicles or 10–12 ice blocks)

Apple:
1 cup plain yoghurt
1 cup stewed apple
1 tbs honey

Combine and freeze.

Banana:
2 medium bananas
1 cup plain yoghurt
1 tsp lemon juice

Mash bananas with lemon juice. Stir in yoghurt and freeze.

Banana and Carob:
2 medium bananas
1 cup plain yoghurt
1 tsp lemon juice
2 tbs carob powder

Mash bananas with lemon juice. Mix yoghurt and carob. Combine and freeze.

Peach:
2 large ripe peaches
1 cup plain yoghurt
1 tsp lemon juice

Puree peaches and lemon juice. Stir in yoghurt. Combine and freeze.

Berry:
2 cups fresh or frozen berries
1 tbs honey
1 cup plain yoghurt

Puree berries and honey. Stir in yoghurt and freeze.

FRUIT JELLIES (Serves 4–6)

1 litre pear or apple juice
2 tbs heaped agar agar or kanten flakes or powder
1 cup raspberries
1 cup blueberries

Place ½ litre juice in a saucepan with the agar agar or kanten, stir and bring to a slow boil. Boil 5 to 10 minutes until agar agar is dissolved, stirring constantly. Add the other ½ litre juice and pour into individual bowls, cool a little, add the berries and allow to set. Top with yoghurt or whipped cream if desired. Note: Agar agar or kanten is a vegetable gelatin. 1 level dsp to a cup of liquid can be used to set any liquid to a jelly. Any fruit or vegetable can be set with this.

¾ cup unsweetened pineapple juice
1 cup water
1 can pineapple pieces
5 tsp agar agar powder

Boil the agar agar in the water stirring constantly until agar agar dissolves. Stir in pineapple juice and roughly chop the pineapple pieces and add to the agar

agar mix as the jelly begins to set. This basic method can be used with most fruit and juices. 1 dsp agar agar to 1 cup of juice. Fold in the fruit after the jelly cools a little, otherwise the fruit will sink to the bottom of the container.

Or cut oranges in half. Scoop out pulp being careful not to break skin. Make jelly and let cool a little before filling the shell with the fruit jelly and allow to set. Cut in half again making ¼ wedges.

HOMEMADE YOGHURT VARIATION—START YOUR OWN

1 cup almonds soaked overnight and chopped
1 cup rejuvelac or water
½ tsp miso if not using rejuvelac
½ cup regular bought yoghurt to hurry the formulation process

Can use rolled or whole oats in place of almonds. Blend the chopped almonds with the rejuvelac or water, add miso if not using rejuvelac, puree till creamy, add the yoghurt and cover, keep in a warm place for 8–10 hours. Soy yoghurt can be made in the same way as dairy yoghurt. Boil then cool to blood heat the desired quantity of soy milk, add 1 cup of previously made or bought yoghurt to each litre of soy milk or purchase a starter powder from a health food shop. Allow to set for 8–10 hours.

ICE CREAM (1)

500 ml grape juice
100 g creamed coconut
3 tbs tahini
2 tbs carob or cocoa powder
1 tsp vanilla essence

Place 1 cup juice, tahini, vanilla essence and carob in a blender. Place other cup of juice in a pan with the creamed coconut and heat gently until coconut melts. Pour into the blender with other ingredients and blend at high speed for 3 minutes. Pour into trays and freeze for 3–4 hours. This recipe has saturated fat, eat sparingly.

ICE CREAM (2)

6 large ripe bananas; break into 3 or 4 pieces
1 tbs honey
4 tbs soy milk powder (Roberts soy compound, not flour)
⅓ cup grape juice
½ cup dates finely chopped
⅓ cup cold pressed oil

Place all ingredients in a blender and blend until smooth. Place in trays and freeze.

OATMEAL CUSTARD PIE

3–4 cups cooked oatmeal, regular porridge oats
1–2 grated apples

1 tsp cinnamon
¼ cup barley malt or ⅓ tsp stevia powder
½ cup toasted oat flakes
¼ cup ground almonds

Brush a pie plate with olive oil, sprinkle bottom and sides with oat flakes. Combine oatmeal, apple, cinnamon, sweetener. Fill pie plate and sprinkle almonds on top. Bake at 180°C for 30 minutes. Cool and serve cut in pieces.

PEACH PIE (no cooking)

3½ pureed peaches (fresh, frozen or canned)
2 fresh peeled and sliced peaches
½ cup agar agar flakes
½ cup water
1 tsp lemon juice
½ cup apple juice

Place pureed peaches in a bowl, arrange the slices of peach in the bottom of a pie plate. Stir the agar agar flakes into the water and juices, put in a saucepan on the heat and stir still boiling, and simmer for 1 minute. Pour the agar agar mix into the pureed peaches and mix well, pour the mix over the sliced peaches, chill for several hours then serve with the raspberry sauce.

Sauce:
1½ cups frozen raspberries
4 tbs fruit juice
1 tbs maple syrup

Puree till smooth.

RICE PUDDING (Serves 2–3)

2 cups water
⅓ cup rice
600 ml soy milk
1 tbs maple syrup
1 tsp cinnamon
1 tsp vanilla essence
2 tbs currants
1 tsp grated lemon rind

Add the rice to the boiling water, simmer for 10 minutes. Drain the rice then return to the pan with the rest of the ingredients, bring to the boil then reduce the heat and simmer for 30 minutes turning frequently till the pudding is thick and creamy.

TOFU CHEESE CAKE (Serves 10–12)

2 cups rolled oats (ground)
½ cup apple juice concentrate
50 g stoned dates chopped
4 tbs lemon juice
Rind of 1 lemon
3 tbs water
350 g packet of firm tofu
150 ml apple juice
1 banana mashed
1 tsp vanilla essence
1 mango peeled and chopped

Lightly grease 18 cm round loose bottomed cake tin. Mix together the oats and apple juice concentrate, press into the base of pan, bake in 160°C oven for

15 minutes. Put the chopped dates, lemon juice, lemon rind and water into a saucepan and bring to the boil. Simmer for 5 minutes until the dates are soft, then mash them roughly. Place dates in a blender or processor with the tofu, apple juice, mashed banana and vanilla essence then process until the mixture is a thick smooth puree. Pour the puree into the prepared base. Bake in a preheated oven 180°C for 30–40 minutes until lightly golden. Leave to cool in the pan then chill before serving. Place mango in blender and process until smooth; serve as a sauce with chilled cheesecake.

Protein 8 g
Calcium 72 mg
Iron 1 mg
Wheat, Dairy and Egg-free

Cakes

SPICED PUMPKIN FRUITCAKE

¾ cup sultanas
1 cup currants
¾ cup chopped raisins
1 cup water
1½ cups cold mashed pumpkin
1 tbs grated lemon rind
¼ cup cold pressed olive oil
1½ cups soy flour
1½ cups rice flour
3 tsp baking powder
1½ tsp cinnamon

¾ tsp nutmeg
2 tbs sugarless apricot jam

Line a deep 20 cm cake tin with 2 sheets of greaseproof paper. Combine sultanas, currants, raisins and water in a pan, bring to the boil. Remove from heat, stir in pumpkin, rind and oil. Cool to room temperature. Stir sifted flours, baking powder and spices into fruit mixture. Spread into tin and bake in moderately slow oven for about 1½ hours. Cover and cool in pan. Turn out when cold, brush top with warmed sieved jam.

No Saturated Fat
No Added Sugar
Dairy, Egg and Gluten-free

APPLE BARS

½ cup rye flour
½ cup soy compound (not flour)
½ tsp salt skip (baking powder substitute)
½ tsp cinnamon
2 large apples grated
2 tsp lemon juice
2 tbs honey

Sift together the dry ingredients. Mix apple, lemon and honey together. Combine wet and dry ingredients, mix well. Pour into a greased 20 cm × 20 cm cake pan. Bake for 20 minutes at 200°C. Cool and cut.

No Saturated Fat
Wheat, Dairy and Egg-free

APPLE CAKE (Serves 8)

4 tsp substitute raising agent or
2 tsp baking powder
225 g flour—eg. 125 g rice flour + 100 g
rye flour or flour of choice
1 tsp cinnamon
1 tsp mixed spice
75 g butter
½ cup honey
3 cups apples chopped
½ cup apple juice

Mix together dry ingredients. Rub in butter. Stir in honey, apples and apple juice, mixture should be moist and sticky. Spread into lightly greased tray. Bake in oven at 170°C for 20 minutes. Cool in the tin.

Whole cake
Calcium 940 mg
Saturated Fat 43 g
Wheat and Egg-free

APPLE FRUIT MUFFINS

1½ cups SR flour—spelt or wholemeal
½ cup apple grated
½ cup currants
1 tsp mixed spice
1 egg beaten
1 dsp lime marmalade or jam of choice
⅓ cup soy milk

Grease 8–10 muffin tins. Mix all ingredients together and place in pans. Bake for 20–25 minutes at 180°C.

APRICOT TOFU SLICE

Base:
1½ cups rolled oats (break up in a blender)
½ cup rice flour
½ cup almond meal
½ cup honey
½ cup wholemeal flour
1 tsp baking powder
125 g unsalted butter melted

Mix all ingredients well and pat into a pan (approx. 18 cm × 24 cm). Bake for 20 minutes at 200°C.

Filling:
500 g tofu
2 cups chopped, dried apricots
¼ cup honey
1 cup soy milk
3 tbs orange rind finely grated

Blend all together well, pour onto base. Bake at 180°C for 25 minutes. Cool, then chill, decorate.

CRUNCHY OATMEAL COOKIES

3 cups oat flakes
2 cups boiling fruit juice
½ cup rice flour or spelt flour
½ cup chopped almonds
1 tbs oil
½ tsp sea salt
1 tsp cinnamon
1 tsp vanilla or almond extract
½ cup raisins

Dry/toast flakes until golden. Pour into a mixing bowl and scald with hot juice. Let sit for 5–10 minutes. Mix with remaining ingredients. Drop table-spoons of dough onto a preheated oiled cookie sheet. Bake at 220°C for 15–20 minutes.

EASTER CAKE

1 cup raisins
2 cups dates roughly chopped
½ cup currants
1 cup fresh breadcrumbs
1½ cups ground almonds
¼ cup orange rind finely grated
¼ cup lemon rind finely grated
2 tsp cinnamon
1 tsp mixed spice
1 tbs lemon juice

Pulse-chop all ingredients in a food processor. You may need to do it in two batches, as the mix will pack together.

Almond/Marzipan Paste:
375 g ground almonds
1 large egg white (or 2 small egg whites)
1½ tbs honey
2 tsp lemon juice—or more if needed, to combine
2 tsp brandy (optional)

Mix all ingredients together, using hands if necessary, no longer than needed to combine. Wrap in greaseproof paper and refrigerate until needed. Place ½ the fruit mix into a lightly greased cake pan. Pat down. Roll out ½ the almond paste to 12–15 cm and place on top of the mixture in pan. Add the rest of the fruit mix. Pat down firmly. Refrigerate for 2 hours. Roll out balance of the almond/marzipan paste. Turn cake out of pan and lay rolled-out marzi-pan paste on the top and crimp the edges. Sides of the cake can be coated with melted carob buds or 70% cocoa dark chocolate. Marzipan top can be decorated with small eggs made from the Easter Egg recipe. Note: Easter Cake recipe can be made into balls. Roll in a mixture of carob powder and almond meal.

Protein 31 g
Calcium 432 mg
Iron 12 mg
Dairy and Egg-free Wheat-free
(if using rice breadcrumbs or spelt)

EASTER EGGS

½ cup almond butter
1 cup raisins
½ cup coconut
1 tbs carob powder
1 tsp honey
½ tsp vanilla

Pulse-chop all ingredients in processor until the mixture holds together. Shape into small eggs and refrigerate until really firm. Can be coated in melted carob buds or 70% cocoa dark choco-late. Melt carob buds or chocolate in a bowl over a pot of simmering water. Dip eggs one at a time and allow to set on greased greaseproof paper.

MUESLI SLICE

2½ cups muesli (break up a little in a food processor)
250 g plain yoghurt
Jam or stewed fruit
1 tsp cinnamon
Extra 1 cup muesli

Combine 2½ cups muesli and yoghurt. Press into 28 cm × 18 cm tray. Cover with fruit or spread. Sprinkle extra cup muesli on top and press down firmly. Bake for 30 minutes at 180°C. Allow to cool in tray for at least 12 hours before cutting into bars.

Protein 42 g
Calcium 371 mg
Iron 14.5 mg
Dairy and Egg-free
(if using soy yoghurt)

NUTTY CARROT CAKE

3 cups carrot finely grated
3 tbs honey
1 cup soy milk or water
250 g tofu
2 tbs olive oil
2 tsp cinnamon
1 tsp mixed spice
1 cup chopped almonds
1 cup sultanas
1 cup wholemeal flour
¼ cup soy flour
4 tsp salt skip baking powder

Blend the carrot, honey, soy milk (or water), oil and tofu until well combined. Mix the cinnamon, mixed spice, nuts, sultanas and flours, then poor in the carrot mixture. Mix thoroughly. Pour into lightly oiled cake tin and bake 180°C until cooked throughout about 40 minutes. Test with a skewer to check if the middle is cooked. Serve hot or cold.

NUTTY FRUIT BARS (Makes 24)

⅓ cup honey
⅓ cup raisins
⅓ cup sunflower seeds
¼ cup chopped pitted dates
¼ cup chopped dried apricots
¼ cup raw nuts
1 cup hulled sesame seeds

Melt honey in pan and stir in rest of ingredients. Mix well and pour into 9" buttered pan. Allow to dry at room temperature for 3–4 hours. Cut into bars.

RICE BRAN AND APRICOT LOAF

1 cup rice bran
½ cup honey or pureed apricots
1½ cups brown rice flour
3 tsp baking powder
1 cup natural yoghurt
1 cup chopped dried apricots

Sift flour and baking powder. Combine bran, yoghurt, chopped apricots and honey. Allow to stand for 10 minutes. Add flour and mix well. Place in a greased loaf pan and bake for approximately 1 hour at 180°C.

SCONES (Makes 10)

Spelt Flour/Savoury

3 cups spelt flour or flours of choice
5 tsp baking powder substitute or 2½ tsp baking powder (or 3 cups of SR flour)
½ cup plain yoghurt
¼–½ cup soy, oat or rice milk
½ tsp Herbamare
¼ tsp chopped rosemary
½ tsp chopped thyme
1 tbs chopped parsley

Sift flour and baking powder into a bowl, add all seasonings. Make a well in the centre and pour in the yoghurt and milk. Mix gently to a soft dough; if mix is crumbly add more milk, turn out onto a floured surface. Pat out to a 3 cm thickness, cut into rounds and place onto a greased oven tray and bake for approximately 15 minutes at 220°C.

Sweet scones

Omit Herbamare and herbs. Add ¾ cup currants and 1 tablespoon of honey (mixed in with milk and yoghurt).

Protein 24 g
Calcium 141 mg
Iron 2.5 mg

Drinks

ALMOND AND HONEY DRINK

¼ cup almonds
2 tsp honey
1 cup water

Whiz for a few minutes in a blender.

HOMEMADE LEMONADE

2 cups lemon juice
½ cup apple juice concentrate

Use as a cordial. 1 tbs per glass. Top up with ice blocks and mineral water. This is still delicious when only water is used to fill the glass.

LEMON AND HONEY DRINK

Mix the juice of 1 lemon
1 tsp honey
1 chopped mint leaf
2 cups water

REJUVELAC (renews the bowel flora)

2 cups wheat berries
1½ litre water

Soak the wheat berries for 24 hours in cold water, drain and then rinse them. Place berries in a jar with 1½ litres of fresh water. Cover the mouth of the jar with a sprout screen or a piece of clean cheesecloth. Let stand for 2 days. Drain off rejuvelac and store, add 1 litre of water to the berries and let stand for 1 day. Then drain off second batch of rejuvelac and add to the first batch, and compost the wheat berries.

SMOOTHIES (Serves 2)

1½ cup milk of choice
2 tbs yoghurt (dairy or soy)
4 dates chopped
½ ripe banana or 4 strawberries

½ tsp vanilla or 1 dsp carob or cocoa powder

Blend ingredients until smooth.

STRAWBERRY SHAKE (Serves 3)

1 cup strawberries
2 tbs apple juice concentrate
2 cups milk of choice
½ cup yoghurt
1 tsp honey

Puree and blend until smooth.

Thrive
Natural Foods

Michelle Russell runs Thrive Natural Foods, her cooking school located in Port Melbourne. Michelle runs courses and classes in natural food preparation to assist people in making the change to a healthier way of eating. She also has the blessing of The Gawler Foundation to offer cooking classes to cancer patients. The classes are packed with simple, delicious food, useful information and organisational tips. The classes can also be done by correspondence. The class manuals are available for purchase and assistance is given through phone consultations. A series of 6 DVDs about the Food Foundation Course are also available.

Phone Michelle on 03 9646 5000 or email her at info@thrivefoods.com.au or look up www.thrivefoods.com.au.

Some recipes from Thrive Natural Foods

BETA SALAD (Serves 2–4)

1 large beetroot grated
1 large carrot grated
Juice of 1 orange
2 tbs flax seed oil
Desiccated coconut

Combine grated beetroot and carrot in a bowl. Dress with the orange juice, flax oil and a sprinkle of coconut. Mix together and serve as an accompaniment to any salad or meal.

This salad is high in beta carotenes which are powerful anti-oxidants. Anti-oxidants help to remove chemicals and harmful free radicals from the body.

RADISH SALAD (Serves 2)

4 red radishes
1 Lebanese cucumber
½ bunch watercress
Splash of flax or olive oil
Splash of mirin (sweet brown rice seasoning)

Chop radishes and cucumber into small cubes. Break watercress off the stems and chop into salad. Dress with oil and mirin. Toss well and enjoy!

Radishes are excellent for the digestion of protein as they stimulate the production of hydrochloric acid. Watercress is high in immune-supporting Vitamin A and great for removing acid mucus wastes from the body. It is also high in calcium. Both radishes and watercress are protective foods. They help to carry toxins from the body.

VEGETABLE CASSEROLE
(Serves 6)

½ head cauliflower cut into small florets
2 zucchini sliced
2 bunches asparagus trimmed and cut into 4 cm lengths
1 red salad onion cut into crescent moons
2 tbs chopped almonds
Salt

Place the cauliflower, salt and onions in 1 cup of water in a large saucepan and bring to the boil. Reduce to a simmer for 10 minutes. Add the zucchini and asparagus, simmering for a few more minutes until tender but still a little crunchy. Drain vegetables, setting aside the cooking liquid. Transfer the vegetables to a casserole dish.

Sauce
2 tbs olive oil
2 tbs brown rice flour
½ cup soy or oat milk
1 cup stock from cooking vegetables
2 cloves garlic minced
Handful of finely chopped fresh basil

Heat the olive oil in a small saucepan, add the garlic and sizzle for a few moments. Add the flour and stir well. Slowly add the vegetable cooking liquid and milk, continuing to stir as the sauce thickens. Season with basil. Add liquid as required to thin the sauce as it simmers. Sauce should be thin enough to pour but thick enough to coat the vegetables. Pour sauce over the vegetables in the dish, sprinkle with almonds and bake for 10–15 minutes, until almonds are lightly browned.

MILLET, DATE AND PUMPKIN PUDDING (Serves 2–4)

1 cup hulled millet, cooked
3 tbs pure maple syrup
4 tbs maize flour (organic from the health food shop)
2 tbs pear juice concentrate
¾ cup fresh dates chopped
1½ cups almond, oat or soy milk
1 cup cooked, mashed jap pumpkin
1 teaspoon cinnamon

Place maize flour, pear juice concentrate and maple syrup in a bowl and mix to a paste. Add dates, mashed pumpkin and cinnamon, mixing well. Add the millet and a little of the milk at a time, mixing until smooth. Pour mixture into an ovenproof baking dish and bake in a moderate oven for approx. 45–50 minutes, until top is golden. Enjoy hot or cold for breakfast, as a special dessert or a nourishing snack.

RICE PUDDING WITH MAPLE PECANS (Serves 4)

2 cups cooked brown rice
1 cup soy, oat or nut milk
2 red apples peeled and finely chopped
2 tbs raisins

4 tbs maple syrup
2 tsp finely grated orange or lemon zest
2 tbs orange or lemon juice
1 tsp cinnamon

Combine rice, milk, zest, apples, raisins and cinnamon in a large saucepan. Bring to the boil. Reduce heat and simmer for 20 minutes, stirring frequently. Add the maple syrup and continue to simmer for 10 minutes. Stir through the orange or lemon juice.

MAPLE PECANS

4 tbs pecans roughly chopped
2 tsp maple syrup
Pinch of ground cinnamon

Dry roast pecans in a skillet over medium heat for 2–3 minutes, stirring constantly. Add the maple syrup and cinnamon and continue stirring for 1 minute. Set pecans aside in a bowl and serve on top of rice pudding.

RICE AND VEGETABLE SUSHI

½ pkt toasted nori sheets (cut in half)
10 × 18 cm long strips of carrot ½ cm thick
5 × 18 cm long strips of green capsicum
10 × 18 cm long strips of cucumber
5 × 18 cm long strips of red capsicum
250 g brown rice
2 tbs chopped ginger
1 tbs horseradish
2 cloves garlic chopped
1½ cups chopped mushrooms
½ cup tamari

Cook brown rice until very soft. Do not rinse with water when cooked, just drain away any excess water, add ¾ cup mirin and stir in well. Spread out on tray and allow to cool. Lightly steam carrots and capsicum. Cook mushrooms in tamari, add garlic, drain off any excess liquid, then puree. Puree ginger and horseradish. Place half pieces of nori on flat surface, three-quarters cover with sticky rice, spread a thin layer of ginger and horseradish then layer of mushrooms, then 1 strip of each vegetable across bottom of nori rice sheet. Roll up and seal, having wet a pastry brush with water and brushed along exposed nori sheet. Cut in 6 pieces and serve with dipping sauce of equal quantities of tamari and water.

INDEX

Additives to avoid   23–24
Basic foods to start   25
Biodynamic produce   11–12
Body needs for minerals   30–32
Body requirements of vitamins   28
Braggs bouillon   48–49
Breads   43
Calcium   18
Calories   18
Carbohydrates   18
Carob   42
Central nervous system   19
Circulatory system   19
Cooking classes   12
Cooking techniques   13–15
Dairy products   42
Digestion   57–58
Digestive system   19
Eggs   40
Excretory system   20
Fish   11 & 43
Flours   43–44
Food combining   57–58
Food principles & practices   9–12
Fruit uses & nutrients   53–56
Fruits   53–56
Grains   32–35
Healing diet   60–61
Healing foods for specific body
   systems   19–21
Healing menu   62–71
Healing properties of grains   34–35
Immune boosting tips   56–57

Immune system   20
Individual food nutrients   26–31
Juice nutrients   18
Juices   16–18
Legumes   35–37
Maintenance Diet   78–79
Milks   25 & 48
Minerals   29–32
Mono diet   59
Muscular system   20
Nutrient charts   72–77
Nutrients   27–29
Nuts & seeds   37
Oils & fats   46–48
Organic food   10–11
Packaged food uses   32–39
Protein   18
RDA   18
Reproductive system   21
Respiratory system   19
Seasonings   49
Seaweeds   37–39
Seed cheese   42–43
Shittake mushrooms   45–46
Skeletal system   20
Soy products   44–45
Sweeteners   41–42
Urinary system   20
Vegetable nutrients & uses   49–53
Vegetables   50–53
Vitamins   28–29
Water   48
Weights & measures   22

Recipes

Breads   121–123
Flaky pie crust   121
Chapattis   122
Pizza   122
Savoury corn loaf   123
Spelt bread   123
Walnut corn bread   123

Cakes   132–136
Spiced pumpkin fruit cake   132
Apple bars   132
Apple cake   133
Apple fruit muffins   133
Apricot tofu slice   133
Crunchy oatmeal cookies   133
Easter cake   134
Easter eggs   134
Muesli slice   135
Nutty carrot cake   135
Nutty fruit bars   135
Rice bran & apricot loaf   135
Scones—savoury   136
Scones—sweet   136

Desserts   127–131
Agar Agar for jam   127
Apple oat pikelets   128
Banana Dessert   128
Bread pudding   128
Frozen fruit treats   129
Fruit jelly   129
Home-made yoghurt   130
Ice–cream   130
Oatmeal custard pie   130
Peach pie   131
Rice pudding   131
Tofu cheese cake   131

Dips, Spreads & Stuffings   124–127
Asparagus Guacamole   124
Bean guacamole   124
Beetroot stuffing   124
Lentil spread   125

Lima bean dip   125
Pesto   125
Raita   126
Savoury crumble topping   126
Stuffing for pumpkin   126
Sweet potato dip   126
Tofu dip   126
Tofu avocado spread   127
Tofu tomato spread   127

Drinks   136–137
Almond & honey drink   136
Homemade lemonade   136
Lemon & honey drink   136
Rejuvelac   136
Smoothies   137
Strawberry shake   137

Dressings   115–116
Coleslaw dressing   115
Flax oil dressing   115
Garlic vinaigrette   116
Honey mustard   116
Mint yoghurt   116
Tofu mayonnaise   116
Tomato basil   116

Fish Recipes   119–121
Fish rolls   119
Gingered fish   119
Salmon & tomato pasta   120
Salmon or tuna pate   119
Salmon sauce rice noodles   120
Tuna casserole   121
Tuna stir-fry   121

Grain & Pulse Recipes   90–96
Baked pumpkins   90
Beans & rice   90
Chickpea & veg party pies   91
Chickpea & vegetable rolls   91
Chickpea loaf   91
Greek-style pilaf   92
Hijiki pie   2

Italian beans   93
Lentil pie   93
Lentil rolls   94
Lima bean loaf   94
Millet and tofu burgers   95
Muesli   95
Porridge   95
Split pea & lentil burgers   96
Sweet & sour chickpeas   96
Tempeh risotto   90

Salads   98–108
Arame salad   98
Asparagus rolls   99
Bean sprout salad   99
Caesar salad   100
Chickpea salad   100
Cold noodle salad   101
Coleslaw   101
Fennel coleslaw   101
Hijiki salad   102
Hot noodle salad   102
Lentil salad   102
Mexican pasta salad   103
Noodle & vegetable salad   103
Red cabbage salad   104
Rice paper rolls   104
Sea vegetable salad   105
Simple beetroot salad   105
Spinach & pumpkin salad   105
Spinach salad with rice   105
Spring salad   106
Sushi rice salad   106
Sweet potato salad   107
Warm potato salad (1)   103
Warm potato salad (2)   108
Warm quanta salad   107
Warm tuna salad   108
Zucchini pasta salad   108

Sauces   117–118
Curries yoghurt sauce   117
Green chickpea pasta sauce   117
Pasta sauce   117
Pizza sauce   118

Sprouted almond sauce   118
Yoghurt sauce   118

Soups   109–115
Bean soup   109
Broccoli & almond soup   109
Carrot & cauliflower soup   109
Cauliflower soup   110
Celery soup   110
Corn dumplings   110
Curried zucchini soup   111
Green soup   111
Lentil soup   111
Miso soup base   112
Noodle soup   113
Parsnip & leek soup   113
Root vegetable soup   113
Simple minestrone soup   114
Spicy tomato soup   114
Spinach soup   114
Sweet potato soup   115

Tempeh & Tofu   95–98
Millet and tofu burgers   95
Chow mien   96
Sliced tofu with ginger   97
Tempeh stir-fry   97
Tofu cutlets   98
Tofu triangles   98

Vegetables   80–90
Corn pie   80
Hot noodle & vegetables   80
Lemon-baked vegetables   81
Mixed rice bake   81
Mushroom stir-fry   81
Mushroom stroganoff   82
Potato cakes   82
Potato pie   82
Hot pot   83
Pumpkin & potato casserole   83
Quinoa loaf   84
Rice & vegetable sushi   140
Rosti   84
Sauerkraut   84

Scalloped sweet potato   95
Spicy potatoes   86
Stuffed potatoes   86
Summer vegetable moulds   87
Sweet corn patties   87
Tomato & onion side dish   87
Vegetable & chickpea curry   88
Vegetable choice pie   88
Vegetable nut loaf   89

Vegetable sausages   89
Zucchini loaf   90
Thrive Natural Foods   138–140
Beta salad   138
Maple pecans   140
Millet date pudding   139
Radish salad   138
Rice pudding   139
Vegetable casserole   139

Notes